INVITATION
TO THE
OLD TESTAMENT

A Short-Term **DISCIPLE** Bible Study

INVITATION
OLD TESTAMENT
TO THE

PARTICIPANT BOOK

Celia Brewer Sinclair
& James D. Tabor

Abingdon Press
Nashville

A Short-Term DISCIPLE Bible Study

INVITATION TO THE OLD TESTAMENT

Copyright © 2005 by Abingdon Press

This book is printed on recycled, acid-free, elemental-chlorine free paper.

Harriett Jane Olson, Senior Vice President of Publishing, and Editor of Church School Publications; Mark Price, Senior Editor; Cindy Caldwell, Development Editor; Leo Ferguson, Designer; Kent Sneed, Design Manager.

07 08 09 10 11 12 13 14 — 13 12 11 10 9 8
MANUFACTURED IN THE UNITED STATES OF AMERICA

Contents

Meet the Writers

CELIA BREWER SINCLAIR is a lecturer in the Department of Religious Studies at the University of North Carolina at Charlotte. She holds degrees from Duke University and Yale Divinity School. She has taught in the fields of Bible and Religion since 1978, first in prep school and since 1992 in college settings.

Celia is a writer of adult curricula for The United Methodist Publishing House, Presbyterian Women (PCUSA), and the Episcopal Diocese of North Carolina. Under the name Celia Brewer Marshall, she is author of three books published by Westminster/John Knox Press: *A Guide Through the Old Testament*, *A Guide Through the New Testament*, and *Genesis*, in the *Interpretation Bible Studies* series.

Celia has two daughters in college. She is married to David Sinclair.

JAMES D. TABOR is Chair of the Department of Religious Studies at University of North Carolina at Charlotte. His main area of textual research is Christian origins, ancient Judaism, with emphasis on the Dead Sea Scrolls. His archaeological field work includes the third Judean Desert Expedition, in which radar ground scan methods were used at Qumran; the survey of Wadi-el-Yabis (Wadi Cherith) in Jordan; research at Masada; new Qumran excavations; and participation in the archaeological excavations at Sepphoris directed by James Strange from the University of South Florida. Dr. Tabor and Dr. Shimon Gibson are the directors of the "John the Baptist" cave at Suba outside Jerusalem. In 2000 they investigated a first-century tomb that contained the only Jewish burial shroud ever found from the time of Jesus. Dr. Tabor serves as chief editor of the *Original Bible Project*, a decade-long effort to produce an annotated historical-linguistic translation of the Bible. Among his publications are *A Noble Death*, coauthored with Arthur Droge (HarperCollins, 1992) and *Why Waco: Cults and the Battle for Religious Freedom in America*, with Eugene Gallagher (Univ. of California, 1995).

An Invitation to This Study

The study you are about to begin is one in a series of short-term, in-depth, small group Bible studies based on the design of Disciple Bible Study. Like the series of long-term Disciple studies, this study has been developed with these underlying assumptions:

- the Bible is the primary text of study
- preparation on the part of participants is expected
- the study leader acts as a facilitator rather than as a lecturer
- a weekly group session features small group discussion
- video presentations by scholars set the Scriptures in context
- encouraging and enhancing Christian discipleship is the goal of study

This participant book is your guide to the study and preparation you will do prior to the weekly group meeting. To establish a disciplined pattern of study, first choose a time and a place where you can read, take notes, reflect, and pray. Then choose a good study Bible.

CHOOSING AND USING A STUDY BIBLE

Again, keep in mind the Bible is *the* text for all short-term DISCIPLE Bible studies, not the participant book; the function of the participant book is to help persons read and listen to the Bible. So because the Bible is the key to this study, consider a couple of recommendations in choosing a good study version of the Bible.

First: The Translation

The recommended translation is the New Revised Standard Version (NRSV). It is recommended for two reasons: (1) It is a reliable, accurate translation, and (2) it is used in the preparation of all DISCIPLE study manuals.

However, any reliable translation can be used. In fact, having available several different translations is a good practice. Some of them include the NIV, NJB, REB, RSV, NKJV, NAB. To compare the many English translations of the Bible before choosing, consider consulting the book *Choosing a Bible: A Guide to Modern English Translations and Editions* by Steven Sheeley and Robert Nash, Jr.

Keep in mind that the *Living Bible* and *The Message*, while popular versions of the Bible, are not considered translations. They are paraphrases.

For this study of the Old Testament, in particular, another recommended study Bible to consider is *The Jewish Study Bible* (Jewish Publication Society TANAKH Translation). Also, consider having on hand one of several recent translations of just the Pentateuch that include helpful commentary on the Hebrew text by leading scholars:

- *The Five Books of Moses: A Translation with Commentary*, edited by Robert Alter (W. W. Norton & Co., 2004)

- *Commentary on the Torah*, by Richard Elliott Friedman (Harper SanFrancisco, 2003)

- *The Five Books of Moses: Genesis, Exodus, Leviticus, Numbers, Deuteronomy* (*The Schocken Bible, Volume 1*), by Everett Fox (Schocken Books, Knopf Publishing Group, 2000)

Second: The Study Features

The recommended Bible to use in any study is, of course, a study Bible, that is, a Bible containing notes, introductions to each book, charts, maps, and other helps designed to deepen and enrich the study of the biblical text. Because there are so many study Bibles available today, be sure to choose one based on some basic criteria:

- The introductory articles to each book or groups of books are helpful to you in summarizing the main features of those books.

- The notes *illuminate* the text of Scripture by defining words, making cross-references to similar passages, and providing cultural or historical background. Keep in mind that mere volume of notes is not necessarily an indication of their value.

- The maps, charts, and other illustrations display important biblical/historical data in a form that is accurate and accessible.

- Any glossaries, dictionaries, concordances or indexes in the Bible are easily located and understood.

All study Bibles attempt, in greater or lesser degree, to strike a balance between *interpreting* for the reader what the text means and *helping* the reader understand what the text says. Study Bible notes are conveyed through the interpretive lens of those who prepare the notes. Regardless of what study Bible you choose to use, though, always be mindful of which part of the page is Scripture and which part is not.

GETTING THE MOST FROM READING THE BIBLE

Read the Bible with curiosity. Ask the questions, *who? what? where? when? how?* and *why?* as you read.

Learn as much as you can about the passage you are studying. Try to discover what the writer was saying for the time in which the passage was written. Be familiar with the surrounding verses and chapters to establish a passage's setting or situation.

Pay attention to the form of a passage of Scripture. How you read and understand poetry or parable will differ from how you read and understand historical narrative.

Above all, let Scripture speak for itself, even if the apparent meaning is troubling or unclear. Question Scripture, but also seek answers to your questions in Scripture itself. Often the biblical text will solve some of the problems that arise in certain passages. Consult additional reference resources when needed. And remember to trust the Holy Spirit to guide you in your study.

MAKING USE OF ADDITIONAL RESOURCES

Though you will need only the Bible and this participant book to have a meaningful experience, these basic reference books may help you go deeper in to your study of Scripture. The "Digging Deeper" box that appears at the end of the commentary section in each session will usually call for consulting one or more of the resources listed below.

- *Eerdmans Dictionary of the Bible*, edited by David Noel Freedman (William B. Eerdmans, Grand Rapids, 2000).

- *Eerdmans Commentary on the Bible*, edited by James D. G. Dunn and John W. Rogerson (William B. Eerdmans, Grand Rapids, MI, 2003).

- *Understanding the Old Testament* (*Abridged Fourth Edition*), by Bernhard W. Anderson with Katheryn Pfisterer Darr (Prentice-Hall, Inc., Upper Saddle River, NJ, 1998).

- *Oxford Bible Atlas, Third Edition* (Oxford University Press, Oxford, 1984).

- *A Theological Introduction to the Old Testament*, by Bruce C. Burch, Walter Brueggeman, Terence E. Fretheim, and David L. Petersen (Abingdon Press, Nashville, TN, 1999).

- *A Guide Through the Old Testament*, by Celia Brewer Marshall (Westminster / John Knox, Louisville, KY, 1989).

- *The Complete Dead Sea Scrolls in English* (*Sixth Revised Edition*), translated by Geza Vermes (Penguin Group USA, East Rutherford, NJ, 2004).

- *The Complete World of the Dead Sea Scrolls*, by Philip R. Davies, George J. Brooke, and Phillip R. Callaway (Thames & Hudson, Ltd., London, 2002).

- *The New Interpreter's Bible: A Commentary in Twelve Volumes* (Abingdon Press, Nashville, TN, 1995–2002). Also available in a CD-ROM edition.

- *The Biblical World in Pictures*, Revised Edition, CD-ROM (Biblical Archaelogical Society).

MAKING USE OF THE PARTICIPANT BOOK

The participant book serves two purposes. First, it is your study guide: use it to structure your daily reading of the assigned Scripture passages and to prompt your reflection on what you read. Second, it is your note-taking journal: use it to write down any insights, comments, and questions you want to recall and perhaps make use of in your group's discussions.

As you will see, the daily reading assignments for each session call for reading the Scripture passages *before* reading the commentary. This is intentional. The commentary is full of references to the assigned readings from the Bible and was prepared by writers who assumed that their readers would be knowledgeable of the week's Scriptures before coming to the commentary. So the recommended approach to this study is to let the biblical writers have their say first.

Introduction

As Christians, we often read the Bible "from back to front." That is, we start with the Gospels, with the message of Jesus and his followers, and then we read back into the Old Testament, usually looking for clues to better understand the New Testament and the claims of our faith. What we can lose sight of is that Jesus of Nazareth lived his life as a Jew. He was immersed in "the law and the prophets," the sacred texts that would become the Hebrew Bible. So in a sense, the story of our faith as Christians really begins with the Hebrew Bible. For that story is where Jesus' story began.

Consequently, in this study, we will read the Old Testament "from front to back." We will begin with Israel's understanding of who they were and who God is, and who they are in relation to God. We will not study the Old Testament as merely the precursor for the New Testament. The Hebrew Scriptures have their own integrity. So we will study the Hebrew Bible for what it says, in and of itself, to discover not simply how these texts have spoken to God's people for centuries, but to learn what these texts have to say to God's people today.

At first glance, the Hebrew Bible may seem daunting, intimidating, or confusing. Its narratives are so big and broad. Its literary styles are so diverse. How should we begin to study it? A first step is to recognize that the Hebrew Bible is composed of a variety of literary genres, or kinds of writing, and that all of these kinds of literature have different goals and different modes of communicating. Moreover, all of these genres arose out of unique historical, social, and cultural contexts. The Hebrew Bible contains a single sweeping story and several narrative cycles involving a particular people, chosen by God, and the ongoing relationship God has with them. Contained within those stories are collections of instruction and teaching—*Torah*, often translated "Law"; poetry—public and individual praises to God as well as public and private laments to God; prophetic speech, in the form of both oracles and criticism of the political and social order; compilations of wise sayings, philosophical reflections, and meditations on life; and apocalyptic visions, vividly imagistic writings looking to God's intervention and victory in this world. A second step is to listen to the particular voices emanating from the texts: calls, promises, commands, and assurances. And another aspect of that listening is to attend to the many responses evoked by those voices found in the text, responses that can function for us today as invitations to our own discipleship.

A third step is simply to ask questions all along the way. Who is this God? *Yahweh* (Hebrew), the Lord God, is the One God of the Jews, the One God of the great traditions arising out of the Ancient Near East (Judaism, Christianity, Islam), the One God whom Jesus worshiped. But what exactly does that mean to those in the story who are trying and (often) failing to be faithful? Who were these ancient people? To what extent were they folks like us? What can we learn from Israel's ever-changing and growing understandings of how God operates, of who this God is, and who Israel is in relation to this God? What are we to make of the theme of God's persistent intent in spite of (not because of) human behavior?

Finally, keep in mind that one of the foundational assumptions of this study is that the stories of God's people called Israel are our stories, too. Of course the world of the ancient Hebrews was a world different from ours. They maintained a fragile existence in an often hostile world. Their lives bore the distinctive marks of the Exodus from Egypt, their settlement of the Promised Land, the Babylonian Exile, the Restoration to Judea, and the development of Second Temple Judaism. But the marks of deliverance, cultural accommodation, exile, and restoration are not unique to the people of Israel centuries ago: be alert for connections between their experiences of faith and ours.

In general, this study is intentionally an *invitation* to engage the Old Testament. On one level, it is an invitation simply to read portions of the Old Testament themselves, becoming immersed for several days in representative samples from a variety of Old Testament voices.

On another level, it is an invitation to examine a number of interpretive perspectives on the Old Testament. The commentary for each session in the participant book (the assigned reading for the sixth day) is part of this process and is supplemented by the video segments presented in the weekly class meeting. Continuing the metaphor of "voices," those read in the Bible and in the commentary will be supplemented by the voices of scholars who will (1) delve deeper into a passage of Scripture, or an issue or theme related to the week's readings, and (2) highlight the relationships between Israel and other Ancient Near Eastern societies as found in extra-biblical literature and law codes, in art and artifacts, in archaeological findings and excavations.

The hope is that these sessions will serve as an invitation to your continued and ongoing study of the Scriptures of both Testaments. The goal of the commentary and the videos is to promote conversation between Bible texts, Bible students, and Bible scholars. The expectation of this study is that hearing these myriad voices will invite you to consider the claims those voices make, on our lives, and on God's behalf.

Expect your study group to help you understand *discipleship* as a response to the message of the Hebrew Scriptures. For only when we hear the voices and responses found in these texts will we discover anew our identity in God, our community with one another, and our calling to serve God's vision for this world.

The Making of the Hebrew Bible

*Assemble the people for me, and I will let them hear my words,
so that they may learn to fear me as long as they live on the earth,
and may teach their children so.*

—Deuteronomy 4:10

INTRODUCTION

At some point in your life, you may have made a New Year's resolution to read the Bible from cover to cover, on your own. Eager to get going, you start at the beginning and read straight through. Your resolve starts to weaken by late February or by Leviticus, whichever comes first. There is simply so much material and so little context for understanding. The notes at the bottom of the pages help—somewhat—so you push on a while longer. As so often happens, your ambition, while well-intentioned, wanes and eventually dissipates. You and your resolution move on, perhaps to another, better way of accomplishing the goal. This study invites you to accomplish what that New Year's resolution set out to do: to integrate reading, understanding, and action in a faithful response to God's call on your life.

In this first lesson you will find yourself reading a variety of biblical voices, or literary genres. You will examine a Creation hymn and a narrative about origins; you will sample types of legal material and wisdom teaching; you will hear the opening chapters to one of Israel's greatest prophets and the poetry of two lovers. These selections represent some of the voices you will hear throughout the Bible. Their variety contributes to the making of the Bible as it comes to you today.

DAILY ASSIGNMENTS

As you read through each passage of Scripture this week, keep in mind the following questions: (1) What are the benefits of having such a variety of different voices to tell the single, sweeping story of God? (2) How do these disparate voices hold together to form a coherent whole? (3) What voices do you listen to more readily or receptively than others? Why is that? (4) Which voices are hard to hear? Why is that? (5) What are the distinctive qualities of this collection of voices that have made possible the faith formation of so many people for so long?

DAILY PRAYER PSALM: Psalm 119:105-112

DAY ONE: Genesis 1–3

Notice two perspectives on Creation. The first (Gen. 1:1–2:4a) is hymnic and stately; the second (which starts with Gen. 2:4b) is a narrative full of suspense. How do the accounts differ? How do they complement each other?

DAY TWO: Leviticus 16–20

Skim the material with this idea in mind: Where we find laws, we find the real concerns of a society. What concerns and interests are reflected in this legal material?

DAY THREE: Proverbs 14–17

Scanning the whole Book of Proverbs will reveal more than one style of writing. Chapters 1–9 contain several long poems, notable for the personification of Wisdom as a woman (9), in contrast to much of the rest of the book's pithy sayings. As you read chapters 14–17, look for common themes. Which proverbs impress you most with their particularly vivid imagery?

DAY FOUR: Jeremiah 1, 2

How does Jeremiah feel about his call to be a prophet? What features of his call do you find most powerful? Most intimidating?

DAY FIVE: Song of Songs 1–4

You are hearing the voices of two lovers. How do they describe each other and their love? How do you feel about the inclusion of this poetry in the biblical canon?

DAY SIX: Commentary

Read the commentary in the participant book.

THE BIBLE:
AN ANTHOLOGY OF BOOKS

The English word *Bible* comes from the Greek phrase *ta biblia*, meaning "the books." This was an expression Greek-speaking Jews used to describe their sacred texts several centuries before the time of Jesus. These books were actually scrolls made from the pithy part of the papyrus stalk, exported from the ancient Phoenician port city of Biblos. Jews call this collection of books the *Tanakh*, an acronym for their three divisions of the Bible: the *Torah*, or Law, also called the books of Moses; the *Nevi'im*, or Prophets, divided into the Earlier and Latter Prophets; and the *Kethuvim*, or Writings, including Psalms, wisdom books, and other diverse literature. Christians adopted the phrase "Old Testament" to refer to those sacred books they shared with the Jews. However, these common books are arranged differently in the Christian canon, using a fourfold division: Pentateuch, corresponding to the Torah; historical books; poetical and wisdom books; and prophetic books. Modern-day scholars use the term "Hebrew Bible" to refer to these sacred books since almost all of them were first composed in Hebrew, the language of Israel. Therefore, the Bible we have today is an anthology of books and diverse literary genres, containing prose, poetry, songs, prayers, folklore, proverbs, prophecy, legal materials, and apocalypses. None of these categories is limited to the Hebrew Bible; all are found in other ancient literature, especially that of the Near East. Materials were written, collected, and edited over a period of a thousand years, though many texts existed much earlier in oral form. The earliest written portions of the Hebrew Bible include the Song of Deborah (about 1100 B.C.), while the latest to be written, Daniel, dates from the second century B.C.

While an officially closed canon of the Hebrew Bible—meaning standard texts of the twenty-four books regarded as authoritative for the community—cannot be spoken of much before A.D. 100, for centuries before, Jewish faith was shaped and nurtured by texts considered to be Scripture. Consider the testimony of the Bible itself on this point: in 2 Kings 22–23, King Josiah finds a "book of the law" in the Temple and leads the people on a campaign of religious reform in the seventh century B.C.; then two centuries later, according to Nehemiah 8–10, Ezra reads from "the book of the law of Moses" to call the community of returned exiles to obedience. While we can only speculate about this long process of authorizing and appropriating sacred writings for ordering Jewish life and worship, we can be sure (and grateful) that the Hebrew Bible, as we have it today, contains a rich diversity of theological themes and literary styles. Our present hearing of these ancient narratives is clearly enriched by having more than one voice tell the story.

HYMNIC CREATION; NARRATIVE CREATION

The first voice we hear in the Bible is singing: a hymn to Creation. The first word of this hymn, *bere'shit*, translated as "In the beginning," is the Hebrew name for the first book of the Torah. Genesis, like most of the other narrative works in the Hebrew Bible, is composed of a number of individual units. These units circulated independently and orally for centuries before they were finally collected. The collection that now stands as Genesis 1–11 contains six major units: two Creation accounts, stories about the expulsion from Eden, Cain and Abel, Noah and the flood, and the tower of Babel. We might picture these units as patches in a quilt. Some patches are older than others; some functioned initially to explain the origin of some place, practice, or name, such as, Where did the rainbow come from? or Why are we afraid of snakes? But seen as a whole, the overarching theme of Genesis 1–11 addresses the question: What is God's relationship to the created order and to us? The answer to that question comes immediately in Genesis 1:1–2:4a. God is Creator of all things, sings the text. This hymn most likely represents a patch of the quilt that originally stood alone. It is a hymn of seven days or stanzas, each stanza except the last ending with the refrain, "And there was evening and there was morning, the [first, second, etc.] day."

The scope of this hymn is the vast cosmos. *Elohim*, the name used here for the One God, calls the created order into being by fiat. God simply speaks: "Let there be . . . ," *Elohim* says. And with each call, *Elohim* proclaims, "It is good." The original stuff of Creation is "the deep" chaos waters, which are driven back by *Elohim*'s command. The stately, deliberate movement from chaos to order begins with the creation of time: "Let there be light," separating

---

There are numerous ways scholars divide the material in Genesis 1–11. Here is another representive outline:

Genesis 1:1–11:26, The Primeval Story

A. 1:1–6:4, The Creation and Disruption of the Universe

   1:1–2:3, The Creation
   2:4-25, Another Look at Creation
   3:1-24, The Intrusion of Sin
   4:1-26, Cain and Abel
   5:1-32, Adam's Family Tree
   6:1-4, Sin Becomes Cosmic

B. 6:5–8:22, The Flood: The Great Divide

C. 9:1–11:26, A New World Order

   9:1-17, God's Covenant with Noah
   9:18-29, Curse and Blessing in Noah's Family
   10:1-32, The Table of Nations
   11:1-9, The City of Babel
   11:10-26, From Shem to Abraham

From *The New Interpreter's Bible, Volume 1, Genesis*, p. 332 (Abingdon Press, Nashville, TN, 1994)

---

the light from the darkness. The movement ends with the crowning glory of God's work as *Elohim* creates humankind. Male and female are created, simultaneously, in the image of God. "And behold, it was very good" (Gen. 1:31).

Genesis 2:4b begins another piece of the quilt, a second perspective on Creation. Instead of a hymn, this patch, which continues through Genesis 3, is a narrative. The scope is limited in time ("the day" of Creation) and focused on three actors: the man, the woman, and God, here called *Yahweh*. (In chapter 3, an antagonist, the serpent, will join the drama.) *Yahweh* is pictured as a potter working with loose earth or dust (Hebrew *'adamah*), the original stuff of Creation. First, *Yahweh* molds an "earth man" (Hebrew *'adam*) from the soil and breathes into his nostrils the breath of life. Next, dry dust is watered into a fertile garden. Then companions are sought for the man. Again, out of the ground, Yahweh forms cattle, animals of the field, and birds. But not finding a fitting partner for the man, *Yahweh* finally forms a woman, the last handmade creation in the narrative.

> **All humanity, male and female, is created in God's image, reflecting the goodness, will, and creativity of the loving, purposeful Creator.**

These two perspectives on Creation complement each other like quilt patches laid side-by-side. They point to the one God who is both transcendent and immanent, beyond all limits (Gen. 1) and yet close at hand (Gen. 2). Creatures are made of dry earth, and to dust they will return (3:19). Yet all humanity, male and female, is created in God's image (1:27), reflecting the goodness, will, and creativity of the loving, purposeful Creator. But in Genesis 3, the story goes on to tell how God's good creation becomes distorted by sin, creating a threefold separation: between God and humans, humans and each other, and humans and the created order.

In these two Creation accounts, hymn and narrative stand side by side in the text. The anonymous "quilters" or editors chose to include both. Together, the hymn and the narrative have a symmetry, a wholeness. Each speaks in its own way about who God is and about who we are in relation to God. Together, the hymn and the narrative represent complementary understandings and mature reflections of Israel's faith.

LEGAL MATERIALS

According to tradition, the will of God was revealed to Israel through Moses when God made a covenant with Moses at Mount Sinai. The Ten

Commandments and the additional legal materials are found in Exodus 20 through the end of the Book of Deuteronomy. This section of the Torah narrates the events at Sinai up to the farewell speech of Moses before the Hebrews entered the Promised Land. The parts of the Law we read in this session come from Leviticus and are concerned particularly with proper sacrifices: gifts of thank offerings, and sacrifices of animals, flour, meal for sin offerings as means of atonement with God. According to these passages, the blood of sacrificed animals literally "covered over" the sin of the people and restored their covenant relationship with God. Included in these Levitical prescriptions for how to maintain covenant purity also were prohibitions against eating blood. These prohibitions reflect Yahweh's (and Israel's) sense of the blood's powerful life force and therefore something not for human consumption.

In reading these legal texts from the Hebrew Bible, keep in mind that though Temple sacrifices have not been offered in nineteen hundred years and Canaanite culture no longer threatens monotheism, the ethical aims of Leviticus are timeless. Recall that the admonition to "love your neighbor as yourself" is first found in Leviticus 19:18. Israel is to remember that they were once strangers in a strange land, and they are to take special care of the sojourners in their land: "You shall love the alien as yourself, for you were aliens in the land of Egypt: I am the LORD your God" (Lev. 19:34). Such words of the Law still speak what God's people need to hear.

THE PROPHETIC VOICE

Having received the Law, the people of Israel struggled to maintain their covenant loyalty to Yahweh, first within a loose tribal confederacy and eventually under the rule of a king. According to the biblical account, Israel's exclusive devotion to Yahweh and obedience to the Law was constantly threatened by accommodation to the surrounding culture. So, with the rise of a United Monarchy, in a time of relative stability, there arose a powerful new voice: a voice sometimes calling the people away from idolatry and back to God, sometimes calling the people to greater obedience and purer worship, sometimes calling the people toward God's purposes for their future. This was the voice of the prophet. In Jeremiah 1 and 2, Jeremiah receives his call to be a prophet and to accept the task God has set out for him. Jeremiah initially refuses the call (1:6). But the prophet (Hebrew *nabi*) appears to have no real choice. There is no such thing as a prophet who wants the job and relishes the task. Jeremiah's call will mean ostracism and persecution. The call means God is engaged in a serious struggle with the people to be heard. The *nabi* becomes a mouthpiece for God—even in times when all seems well. In Jeremiah's case, his prophetic voice enacts judgment and parallels the Lord's actions: it will terrify and tear down; later it will build up and restore. The Southern Kingdom of Judah will fall to the Babylonian Empire during Jeremiah's watch despite his urgent warnings and cries for change. Later there will be a return from exile and a renewed covenant.

> **Crisis is the classic context for hearing the prophetic voice in Scripture, and its favorite tense is the present.**

Crisis is the classic context for hearing the prophetic voice in Scripture, and its favorite tense is the present. The prophet declares that, here and now, changes must occur. The future is open and contingent; disaster can be averted if only the people will remember the covenant and mend their ways. Jeremiah's task, as is the task of the other biblical prophets, is to cajole and shout until God's people hear and obey. But God's people do not hear and obey. Their faithlessness persists. So the voice of the prophet persists even more, highlighting one of the distinctive characteristics of this voice in the Bible: its vital redundancy.

VOICES OF WISDOM

The voices of wisdom in the Bible include both collections of short wisdom sayings and aphorisms, as in the Book of Proverbs, as well as long compositions such as Job and Ecclesiastes. In all three of these wisdom writings, the very human voice we hear is one that ranges wide in its subject matter. The voice in Proverbs offers very practical advice for living a good and successful life. The voice of Qohelet in Ecclesiastes meditates on the meaning of life and the finality of death, and argues in favor of a fairly cynical perspective on the ultimate meaning and purpose of God's ways. The voice of Job agonizes over the question of the suffering of the righteous and how to understand God, given the reality of such suffering.

Though the voices of Israel's wisdom traditions can sound very different, they all share some basic features. First, many of their themes are reminiscent of texts originating from other Ancient Near Eastern cultures such as Egypt and Mesopotamia. Wisdom literature, particularly didactic proverbs and moralistic fables, were some of the earliest forms of writings. Second, the wisdom books in the Old Testament are not concerned with rehearsing the history of Israel; they are more interested in making sense of God, Creation, and the place of human beings in the cosmic order. Third, the plain realities of life and death, especially the mysteries of pain and suffering, are wisdom's recurring refrains. And finally, Israel's wisdom writings usually aim to teach a lesson, promote virtuous behavior, or clarify the limits of what a person can know about human destiny and God.

POETIC VOICES

The five relatively short books of Song of Songs, Ruth, Lamentations, Ecclesiastes, and Esther are collectively known as the Five Scrolls. These scrolls are read over the course of the year in many Jewish communities and in the synagogue on holidays, beginning with the Song of Songs on Passover. The Song of Songs is a poetic exchange between two lovers. Traditionally, the authorship was ascribed to Solomon, which no doubt gave the book added authority. However, the primary voice is that of a young unnamed woman, "black and beautiful," who addresses her beloved. Scholars differ on the original form or function of the poem. It may have been a drama with characters (a woman, a man, and a chorus of the daughters of Jerusalem) speaking their lines. The descriptions in the poem bear some resemblance to Arabic love poetry. The poem is fragmented and sometimes difficult to follow, perhaps because it represents several different poems or simply because parts are missing. The overt eroticism of this book has led some Jewish and Christian interpreters to read it, not as love poetry, but as an allegory of the mutual love of God and Israel, of Christ and the church, or of the relationship of the worshiper to God. Such an allegorized or "spiritual" reading makes erotic language an appropriate way to express religious devotion in the Western tradition, both in Jewish and Christian readings. The inclusion of the Song of Songs within the canon is an affirmation of the essential created goodness of the body and of romantic desire. The woman's voice, presented in the first person rather than through a narrator, is what scholar Renita Weems calls "the only unmediated female voice in Scripture," a candid and outspoken expression of joy for the lover, a celebration of sexual love between humans.

INVITATION TO DISCIPLESHIP

Isaiah 55 contains a profound promise: just as the rain and snow come to earth to nourish it, God's Word comes to us for the same purpose. And just as the rain does not return to heaven before accomplishing its purpose, neither will these Scriptures return to God before they accomplish their purpose. In other words, God expects these Scriptures to germinate in the hearts of those who "seek the Lord while he may be found" (Isa. 55:6). God expects these texts to say something important to us. The question for us is how can we have that same expectation of Scripture when we come to it? Or to ask it another way, how do we listen to the various voices in the Old Testament so that we accurately hear what God is saying?

One of this study's recommended resources is *A Theological Introduction to the Old Testament* (see bibliography on p. 10 of the participant book). In that book the authors emphasize the importance of recognizing the twin gifts of diversity and continuity the Old Testament offers its readers:

> No one who has read the Old Testament can fail to notice the great diversity of voices that speak through its texts. Narrative and poetry, peasant piety and royal archive, priestly ritual and pro-phetic utterance, apocalyptic vision and wisdom saying—all of these voices and many more witness to the polyphonic nature of the Old Testament as a whole. It is one of the great gifts of the Old Testament as a theological resource to the community of faith that almost any person in any role or circumstance can find a voice within the Old Testament witness that seems to offer the reader common ground. . . .

Let us be on the lookout then, for common ground as we travel the way of faith together. Let us listen carefully. For the story of Israel's God is the story of our God; and Israel's struggle to be God's people is our struggle.

FOR REFLECTION

• Read aloud Deuteronomy 4:10. In light of your study this week, how does this verse reflect the theme of the Scriptures you read? How is the voice of the text calling you to respond?

• Of the variety of voices in this week's readings, which one most challenges your understanding of the message of the Old Testament? Why?

• In the sweep of Israel's story in the Old Testament, where do you find common ground?

DIGGING DEEPER

Read articles in a Bible dictionary about the Dead Sea Scrolls, the Septuagint, and the Masoretic text of the Hebrew Bible. Consider what these textual sources contribute to our study of the Bible we use today.

Use the space below to make notes, identify questions, and jot down your thoughts for use during the weekly group meeting.

The Creation Story of Israel

I will bless those who bless you, and the one who curses you I will curse; and in you all the families of the earth shall be blessed.

—Genesis 12:3

INTRODUCTION

Family: Can't live with them, can't live without them. Our families shape who we are, become the first connections we make, and provide the most important ties that bind. They can, at times, be both difficult and nurturing, full of rivalries and full of sympathies, sources of heartache and of the deepest joy.

The texts this week are concerned with families, the primary social units in biblical culture. The call and creation of the chosen people, Israel, is commonly known as the "patriarchal history" with the patriarchs being Abraham, Isaac, and Jacob. God begins the relationship with this people by initiating a covenant with Abraham and Sarah that will be passed down from them to generation after generation. God chooses to enter into the rivalries, favoritisms, commitments, and misunderstandings that characterize these first families of the covenant. God's promises work toward the continuation of these families, bringing the miracle of birth to barren women and providing for the future of Israel. God's presence is also involved in familial conflict and intrigue.

The stories of the patriarchs and matriarchs constitute a "creation narrative" of the chosen people. Israel understood itself to begin, at a particular time and place, with God's call of Abraham. This call and these people are the sources for understanding who Israel is and who God is.

DAILY ASSIGNMENTS

These stories point to Israel's origins, but they also contain truths for us today. We find ourselves in these stories. As you read through each passage of Scripture this week, keep in mind the following questions: (1) What obstacles does God experience with the choice of this particular family? (2) How does your family system compare to that described in these readings? (3) How is "family" the important metaphor for the covenant relationship with God?

DAILY PRAYER PSALM: Psalm 105:1-11

DAY ONE: Genesis 11:27–12:20; 15

What promises does the Lord make to Abram and Sarai (later renamed Abraham and Sarah)? The Lord repeatedly says, "I am . . ." and "I will. . . ." What does God reveal in these descriptions and predictions?

DAY TWO: Genesis 16–18; 21–22

What do you learn about Abraham from these episodes? Draw a family tree for Abraham, Sarah, Hagar, Ishmael, and Isaac. Include the blessings God gives each member of the family.

DAY THREE: Genesis 24; 25; 27; 28

In these readings, Isaac is a shadowy figure while Rebekah moves the action along. Note how she shows initiative and energy. How is she attuned to the will of God?

DAY FOUR: Genesis 29–30

Continue drawing the family tree, adding Rebekah, her sons Jacob and Esau, and Jacob's wives and children. Include blessings given by God to each.

DAY FIVE: Genesis 31–33

What do you learn about Jacob from these episodes? His new name, Israel, means "one who struggles with God." How is this name fitting for Jacob? How is the name fitting for other patriarchs and matriarchs in Genesis?

DAY 6: Commentary

Read the commentary in the participant book.

THE THREEFOLD PROMISE

The sweeping scope of Genesis 1–11 narrows to a pinpoint, to a single family, with Genesis 12. "Go," God tells Abram. The good news is that Abram heard and acted. Extraordinary promises are made. Go to the land I will show you, God says, and there I will do three things: I will give you all the land that you see; I will make of you a people; and through you all the nations will be blessed. This covenant is unilateral and unconditional. A land, a people, and a blessing to the world are promised to Abram and his descendants.

Together Abram and Sarai travel from Sumer (modern Iraq) across Mesopotamia for one thousand miles before reaching Shechem, a Canaanite town near the center of the Holy Land. Abram could not have known what this God, whom he called El Shaddai (God of the mountain) and El Elyon (Most High God), was all about. He answered the call immediately, inexplicably, faithfully. But Abram had much to learn. The journey through Mesopotamia, across time and space, is a metaphor for the journey Abram made into the covenant with this hitherto unknown God.

God tells Abram, "In you all the families of the earth shall be blessed" (Gen. 12:3). The creation story of Israel begins with a particular relationship to a particular people. But this covenant is not an end in itself. It is not simply a matter of being chosen. Israel is God's "first-born" child in a huge family. As the first-born, it is Israel's responsibility to model the best of what covenantal relationship means to the rest of the family of nations (see Amos 3:2 and Exod. 19:5). The covenant benefits are at first focused on Israel; but their scope is without limits.

God reminds Abram again and again of what God intends for the future. The threefold promise is reiterated in Genesis 15 and 17. "Look toward heaven and count the stars. . . . So shall your descendants be" (15:5). In a mysterious ceremony, with smoking torches and terrifying darkness, God seals the covenant with animal sacrifices (15:9-11). God renames Abram's wife: Sarai, "my princess," will henceforth be called Sarah, or "the princess of multitudes" (17:15). God says, "I will bless her, and moreover I will give you a son by her. I will bless her, and she shall give rise to nations; kings of peoples shall come from her" (17:16). Abram ("exalted father") is renamed as well. Henceforth he will be Abraham, "father of a multitude of nations" (17:5).

Abraham laughs at God's pronouncement. He cannot believe that a baby will be born to parents who are past childbearing years. So Abraham reminds God of his son by Hagar: "O that Ishmael may live in your sight!" (Gen. 17:18).

But God persists and reiterates that Sarah will give birth to a son who will inherit the covenant.

God makes it clear that Abraham and Sarah are covenantal partners. It is their son who will inherit the blessing. Isaac, the child of laughter and their old age, is the sign to Sarah and Abraham that God's promises will be worked out in spite of their long childlessness. God works through them as partners. Such was God's intent all along.

> **Isaac, the child of laughter and their old age, is the sign to Sarah and Abraham that God's promises will be worked out ... through them as partners.**

THE NEXT GENERATION

The dominant motif in Sarah's life, besides her marriage to Abraham, is her inability to have children. When she is first introduced in Genesis 11:30 we are told, "Now Sarai was barren; she had no child." God's promise of descendants, as many as the stars in the sky or the sands on the shore, seems problematic.

Sarah knows three things: her marriage to Abraham, her barrenness, and God's promise. All three are important to her, but all three cannot coexist. Sarah works toward actualizing the covenant by taking the key role in solving the problem of barrenness. "Go in to my slave-girl; it may be that I shall obtain children by her," she tells Abram in Genesis 16:2. Perhaps, she says, I will be "built up" through this birth. The custom was for the surrogate mother to deliver the baby "on the knees" of the wife, who would then raise the child as her own. Such was Sarah's plan as she attempted to realize the promise. However, this slave woman becomes an issue. Her name, which Sarah never uses, is Hagar. Initially, she was an acceptable means to an end for Sarah. But something went horribly awry, and jealousy drives a wedge between them.

The first time Hagar is driven into the wilderness, she is pregnant. God appears to her and tells her to return so that the child she is bearing will survive. Both she and her child are promised a future. God makes a pledge to the slave girl: "I will so greatly multiply your offspring that they cannot be counted for multitude" (Gen. 16:10).

The second time Hagar is driven into the wilderness, both mother and son raise their voices in pain. Hagar hears the voice telling her: "Be not afraid" (21:17). God gives her vision to see resources that she had not seen before.

She discovers a well of water in the desert. Ishmael will survive. Keep him safe, God tells Hagar, "for I will make a great nation of him" (21:18). Hagar will become the desert matriarch, mother of desert dwelling Arab tribes and matriarch of Islam. Hagar's son, Ishmael, will become the father of many nations while Sarah's Isaac will inherit the covenant. They have much in common. Both boys shared the same father. Both are children of promise. As youngsters they have not yet learned to be separate, to mirror hostility. But to Sarah, their laughter as they play together (21:9) is a threat. She does not yet fully grasp the breadth of God's promise or God's capacity for hospitality.

THE AKEDAH

In some ways Isaac is merely a bridge between his father, Abraham, and his son, Jacob. He receives the covenant and passes it on. He is otherwise a mystery. We read little about him after the story in Genesis 22—variously called "The Testing of Abraham" and "The Binding of Isaac" (in Hebrew *akedah*, the word for "binding")—and learn little about him from the episode itself. The Bible does not indicate that Isaac either saw or spoke to his father again after the *akedah*. They made the descent from Mount Moriah separately. This problematic passage has an interesting epilogue. There is also no mention of Abraham seeing Sarah again. Her death is recorded just two verses after the *akedah* (Gen. 23:2). After Abraham dies, Ishmael and Isaac together bury him alongside Sarah at the cave of Machpelah near Hebron (Gen. 25:9). The half brothers Ishmael and Isaac, estranged as children, separated from each other by the ill will of their parents, together bury Abraham. In the end they share a commonality that did not exist while their father was alive. Further, they reunite Abraham and Sarah at the Machpelah gravesite. God's promises work toward reconciliation and reunion in spite of the conflict and disunity that prevailed all too often in their family lives.

> ## The Akedah
>
>
>
> According to Jewish tradition, the sacrifice of Isaac is called the *Akedah* (Hebrew for "binding"), and is considered the last of the ten tests of Abraham's faith. The 12th century Jewish sage, Maimonides, identified the ten tests as follows:
>
> 1. Call to leave homeland (Gen. 12:1)
> 2. Famine in Canaan (Gen. 12:2-10)
> 3. Abduction of Sarai (Gen. 12:14-20)
> 4. War with four Kings (Gen. 14)
> 5. Marriage to Hagar (Gen. 16:1-3)
> 6. Circumcision (Gen. 17:1-14)
> 7. Second abduction of Sarah (Gen. 20)
> 8. Banishment of Hagar (Gen. 21:8-14)
> 9. Banishment of Ishmael (Gen. 21:8-14)
> 10. The binding of Isaac (Gen. 22:1-19)

THE MATRIARCH REBEKAH

In Genesis 24, Abraham decides to find Isaac a wife back in Haran, the home of his family and far away from the Canaanite peoples. Being old, Abraham sends his loyal servant on the errand who devises a plan of his own. The servant decides to go directly to the local well, the meeting place of the Ancient Near East, and ask a woman to draw water for him. If she does so and offers to water the camels as well, the candidate for betrothal will have passed the test. Rebekah does just that. She acts quickly, bringing water for both the servant and for the camels. She shows herself to be a young woman of energy and courage. To the question of whether she will go back with the servant, she answers her family simply, "I will." She understands that a great journey awaits her. Upon her arrival and after seeing Isaac from afar, she takes the initiative, veils herself, and comes to him. Isaac takes Rebekah as his wife and loves her (24:67).

After twenty years of childlessness, Rebekah becomes pregnant with twins and a struggle begins. The long-awaited pregnancy is a difficult one for her. The turmoil within is painful: "Why do I live?" (25:22). She seeks out God to ask directly what is happening in her life. The oracle she receives is powerful, direct, surprising. God reveals to her that she will bear two nations, two peoples who will be divided; and the younger one will prevail over the older, stronger one. It is Rebekah who knows her own mind, who knows the mysterious plan of God, and who takes the initiative to act to realize God's purpose.

> **It is Rebekah who knows her own mind, who knows the mysterious plan of God, and who takes the initiative to act to realize God's purpose.**

Likely Isaac was unaware of the oracle. The system of primogeniture, succession by the eldest son, was the common practice in Ancient Near Eastern cultures. The oldest would always inherit a "double portion" (see also Deut. 21:15-17). Certainly Isaac prefers the older Esau to the second-born Jacob. Esau grows up to be man of the field and the hunt, a better fit in his father's mind to be the heir.

The story of Jacob's deception (Gen. 27) is, on one hand, an episode of trickery and intrigue. But seen from Rebekah's vantage point, we note how quickly she acts to bring about what she knows must happen. Convention must be overturned, and in haste. She urges Jacob, "Obey my word as I command you" (27:8). She uses skins to cover Jacob's arms so that he might receive the blessing by tricking Isaac into bestowing his blessing on him rather than Esau. Rachel's plan works, and Isaac's intentions to leave his inheritance to Esau are thwarted. His blessing cannot be taken back. Later, when she hears that Esau intends to murder his brother, Rebekah again tells Jacob, "Obey my voice" (27:43). She sends him to her brother Laban, back in Haran and out of harm's way. She knows the struggle between sons to be the struggle between nations. She draws her own conclusions and devises a strategy, working to preserve Jacob, the promise, and the future.

THE FAMILY GROWS

At this low point in his life, the fugitive Jacob is visited by God. In a dream, Jacob sees a vision of a ladder (or stairway or ramp) pointing to the heavens. Once again, the threefold promise is outlined (Gen. 28:13-15), and now it is passed on to Jacob, the least likely of recipients. Jacob does not deserve it; nevertheless he is heir to the covenant.

The scene shifts to Haran in upper Mesopotamia or Paddan-aram (Gen. 29). Jacob arrives at the home of Laban, his uncle. His first stop is the watering well where he immediately falls in love with Laban's youngest daughter, Rachel. A shrewd businessman, Laban notes the opportunity to get many years of labor from his love-struck nephew before allowing him to marry Rachel. Jacob worked seven years for Rachel's hand, only to discover at the ceremony that the veiled woman he married was Leah. In another kind of ancient primogeniture, the eldest daughter is always first to marry! At the end of the wedding week, Laban gives him Rachel as well, in return for another seven years of indentured labor.

However, the situation becomes untenable. Rachel and Leah are sisters married to the same man. And they live in a society where a woman's worth depends on her ability to bear children. Rachel has Jacob's heart, but no children. Leah has many sons, but not her husband's love. At issue is how their struggles will play out, given the limits of their world together.

ISRAEL IS NAMED

After twenty years, God tells Jacob and his burgeoning family to return to Canaan, the land of his ancestors (Gen. 31:3). On the eve of their entrance into Canaan, Jacob struggles with a mysterious visitor until dawn breaks (Gen. 32:24-32). He demands a blessing from this stranger, and he is re named "Israel." The name is a combination of the Hebrew root for "contend, persist, have power, persevere" and *El*, or "God." Jacob's new name carries multiple senses: "He who will be great before God," "He who contends with God," "He who struggles with the divine." To be Israel is to struggle with God, and with humans, persistently and powerfully. Looking back on the wrestling match, Jacob knows that he has "seen God face to face" (32:30).

The next day, in anxious expectation of a confrontation with Esau, Jacob sends gifts of livestock to his estranged brother. Jacob is prepared for the worst. What he receives instead is the embrace of reconciliation from Esau. A shocked and relieved Jacob declares, "To see your face is like seeing the face of God—since you have received me with such favor" (33:10).

INVITATION TO DISCIPLESHIP

The stories of Israel's origins show the struggles of families with each other and with God. These narratives depict humans candidly, with all of their confusion, their hopes and fears, and at both their best and worst. God chooses to enter into a covenant with this particular people called Israel. God leads them across time and space into a future promising blessing for all the families of the earth. The overarching theme of these narratives is the persistence of God's promises in spite of, and on behalf of, God's chosen people. The Bible emphasizes that God chooses—again and again—to be in loving, covenantal relationship with these people.

In spite of the conflict and disunity that characterize human existence, God promises to work among us toward reconciliation, meaning reconciliation with God as well as with each other.

Consider the matriarchs and patriarchs who took the initiative and acted solely on God's word, stepping out in faith with boldness in an often unknown world. Consider Jacob's story and its portrayal of struggle with God as an occasion for blessing. Consider that in spite of the conflict and disunity that characterize human existence, God promises to work among us toward reconciliation, meaning reconciliation with God as well as with each other. Although our ways often promote division, God's ways more often seek reunion. The Bible tells us so.

And what is our response? Part of our response should be how we as God's people understand our roles as members of our own family and members of God's "family" through Abraham. What is there to learn from these narratives about both the joys and struggles of living faithfully as family?

FOR REFLECTION

- Read aloud Genesis 12:3. In light of your study this week, how does this verse reflect the theme of the Scriptures you read this week? How is the voice of the text calling you to respond?

- How does the knowledge that God's promises are true, as revealed through these narratives, empower and equip you to live more faithfully as one of God's people?

- God promises Abraham and Sarah descendants who will become a great nation. God makes the same promise to Hagar and Ishmael. What does that say about God?

DIGGING DEEPER

Look up the word *El* in a Bible dictionary (*Eerdmans Dictionary of the Bible*, pp. 384–386) or other source (*Understanding the Old Testament*, Anderson, pp. 41–42). Make notes on the origins of the word and its use in the Hebrew Bible. How does knowing about the origins and various meanings of *El* inform your understanding of its usage in the story of Abraham?

Follow the route Abraham took from Ur "by stages toward the Negeb" on a map (*Oxford Bible Atlas*, pp. 54–55). Get a sense of the distance Abraham traveled and the terrain he encountered.

Out of Bondage

*Even though you intended to do harm to me, God intended it for good,
in order to preserve a numerous people, as he is doing today.*

—*Genesis 50:20*

INTRODUCTION

The narratives in this lesson show the realization of the threefold promise first made to Abraham and Sarah. The twelve sons of Jacob grow to twelve tribes in Egypt, beginning with God's providential care of Joseph and Joseph's subsequent provision for his siblings there during the famine. Turn the page from Genesis 50 to Exodus 1 and four hundred years have passed. The flourishing Hebrew tribes are now enslaved in Egypt. God hears their cries and calls Moses to bring them out of bondage and lead them back to Canaan, the land of promise.

The drama of the Exodus event and the revelation of Torah at Mount Sinai are the two most pivotal texts of the Hebrew Scriptures. They recount and celebrate not only a story of liberation but also one of creation: God acts on behalf of a people to free them from bondage; then God speaks the covenant community into being. Initially, the people respond to God's voice with enthusiasm: "All that the LORD has spoken we will do" (Exod. 24:7). But as it becomes apparent later, their response falters—repeatedly, in fact. As the story unfolds in the Book of Numbers, the Hebrews are poised to enter Canaan but are also dispirited and disabled by their years of slavery. The people's entrance into the Promised Land is delayed another forty years. Finally, a new generation, one born of wandering and in freedom, eventually inherits the "land flowing with milk and honey" (Exod. 3:8).

DAILY ASSIGNMENTS

Journeying from the brick-making fields of Egypt to the wilderness of Sinai, a multitude of Hebrews, delivered by Yahweh and led by Moses, becomes a people called Israel. As you read through each passage of Scripture this week, keep in mind the following questions: (1) What is happening to the threefold promise first made to Abraham and Sarah in these readings? (2) The Exodus event is pivotal in the history of Israel. What is it about the event that makes it crucial? (3) What happens to the Israelites once they are freed from slavery? How might you account for their difficulties?

pg 435

DAILY PRAYER PSALM: Psalm 78:12-24

pg 95

DAY 1: Genesis 37; 39–45; 50

Note the portrayal of Joseph from tedious teenager to powerful grown man. In what ways does he recognize that God is with him?

pg 36

DAY 2: Exodus 1–5

Pay special attention to the ways Moses is described as a remarkable person. Then look for evidence of his ordinary humanity in the readings, too.

DAY 3: Exodus 11–15

How would you describe what is special about the night of Passover? How is it to be commemorated?

DAY 4: Exodus 19–20; Deuteronomy 5–6

What laws apply specifically to worship and to the human relationship to God? What laws apply specifically to ethics and human relationships with one another?

DAY 5: Exodus 32–34; Numbers 13–14 *read*

Why do you think Aaron acted as he did in Exodus 32? Characterize the responses of both God and Moses to the golden calf episode in Exodus and to the rebellion at Kadesh in Numbers.

DAY 6: Commentary

Read the commentary in the participant book.

INTO EGYPT:
THE JOSEPH STORY

In a way, the Joseph narrative of Genesis 37–50 serves as a transition between the saga of Abraham and his family's journey to Egypt and the drama of Moses and the Hebrews' escape from Egypt. Some scholars suggest that the settlement of the Hebrew people into Egypt may have coincided with the Hyksos Dynasty (1674–1567 B.C.), a regime known for being hospitable toward Semitic peoples, and whose capital, Avaris, was located near "the land of Goshen." The tale of Joseph reads like a short story told with artfulness, economy of character, and clarity of purpose. Joseph, Rachel's first-born and Jacob's favorite son, is introduced as a young man who is blessed with dreams. He is also guilty of glaring blind spots. He has no sense of how his behavior provokes others, how he infuriates his siblings, how his favored status is perceived by his brothers. They work the fields while he is at home wearing a coat fit for a prince. Twice he reports the content of his dreams to his brothers, leaving no question as to their symbolism and meaning. He dreams that they will bow down to him. Little wonder that his brothers despise him and plot his demise.

By the time the events in Joseph's dream are fulfilled, years have passed and Joseph has changed. We are meant to delight in his character development. He undergoes trials, passes tests, suffers, and succeeds. Sold into slavery by his brothers, he winds up in Egypt as a dependable household servant to Potiphar, the captain of Pharaoh's guard. Framed by Potiphar's amorous wife, he ends up in prison. There he interprets dreams with the awareness that the gift is God's, but he languishes in prison. When Pharaoh needs an interpreter, Joseph is at last remembered, and Pharaoh immediately elevates him to a position of power in Egypt—second only to Pharaoh himself—and orders his people to bow down to this foreigner. God's covenantal promise to Abraham that other nations would be blessed through his descendants is realized in Joseph as he successfully prepares Egypt for a long famine. The famine sends the brothers to Egypt for food and into Joseph's hands. Unaware that their long-lost brother is in control, they helplessly watch as Joseph imprisons Simeon, inflicting on him the same ordeal Joseph had suffered. Joseph also frames Benjamin, Rachel's second son, for theft and threatens him with imprisonment. In one of the most moving speeches in Scripture, Judah offers his own life in place of Benjamin's. The brothers successfully pass Joseph's tests, demonstrating the changes they too have undergone. Never again will they cause the pain of loss to their father, Jacob. The tearful (and, no doubt for the brothers, fearful) reunion of Joseph and his family is the centerpiece of the short story.

Remarkably, there is almost no mention of God in the Joseph narrative. When in prison, Joseph does declare to the butler and the cup-bearer that he is able to interpret their dreams because "interpretations belong to God" (Gen. 40:8). But the overarching motif of the entire story is not Joseph's gift for dream interpretation, but God's providential care. God will find a way—in spite of the mean-spirited, murderous intent of his brothers, and through the dead ends of exile, imprisonment, and famine. Joseph articulates this theological certitude at two points in the narrative. The first occurs when he finally reveals his identity to his brothers (Gen. 45:7-9). He acknowledges that God sent him to Egypt and gave him authority so that he could save many, including his own family, from starvation. The second occurs after Jacob's death (Gen. 50:20-24). The brothers suspect that Joseph may still harbor a grudge toward them and be poised to retaliate. So in the name of their father, they beg Joseph to forgive them. Joseph assures his brothers that they have nothing to fear: "Do not be afraid! Am I in the place of God? Even though you intended to do harm to me, God intended it for good, in order to preserve a numerous people, as he is doing today." Joseph thus affirms God's care and protection and God's intention to fulfill his promises by bringing the people back to the land he swore to Abraham, Isaac, and Jacob. These two short speeches make explicit the work of God that drives the narrative. They state succinctly that God is the real protagonist of the drama. God is finally the one in control. Through Jacob, all of the sons receive blessing by the end of the cycle. The threefold promise is intact.

OUT OF EGYPT: MOSES AND THE EXODUS

After being reunited with his brothers, Joseph brought his entire family to live in the Goshen region of Egypt, a fertile area in the eastern Nile delta. The promise of descendants to Abraham is enacted as the family of Jacob/Israel grows into a sizable clan. They prospered at first, but a shift in power marked the end of the Hyksos Dynasty and brought in Egyptian kings with unfavorable attitudes towards outsiders. The Promised Land remained elusive. When the story picks up in

Hyksos Dynasty

The term *Hyksos* means "rulers of foreign countries," and refers to a West Semitic people who invaded Egypt around 1720 B.C. The Hyksos established a capital city at Avaris, and ruled the Egyptian Empire, including Palestine and Syria, during the Fifteenth and Sixteenth dynasties.

Exodus 1, we find the Hebrews (translated from the word *ibri*, meaning "one from beyond") are enslaved, a people in exile.

The Book of Exodus can be divided into two main parts: sources describing the exit from Egypt (chapters 1–18) and sources focusing on Yahweh's revelation at Mount Sinai (chapters 19–40). While tradition names Moses as the author of Exodus, scholarly consensus is that the book contains a number of sources that have been redacted, or edited, together long after the events described in the text. Whoever compiled the Book of Exodus, they made clear that Israel exists by the power and deliverance of Yahweh as seen in the Exodus event and by the mutually binding character of the Mosaic covenant delivered on Mount Sinai: "You have seen what I did to the Egyptians, and how I bore you on eagles' wings and brought you to myself. Now therefore, if you obey my voice and keep my covenant, you shall be my treasured possession out of all the peoples" (Exod. 19:4-5).

The story of the Exodus opens with Moses' infancy narrative, told against the fearful backdrop of Pharaoh's attempted ethnic cleansing. The Hebrew population threatens him, and he fears that the slaves will revolt. Pharaoh orders the Hebrew midwives to kill all Hebrew boys at birth, but these ingenious women explain that they arrive at Hebrew birthings too late to carry out the letter of the law. Cast the babies into the Nile, he orders. And so Moses is put into a basket rather than being drowned and floats down the river to rest at the place where Pharaoh's daughter rescues him. He is raised in the Egyptian court with Jochebed, his mother, as nursemaid. In spite of Pharaoh's murderous intent, Moses is safely reared under his very roof.

The textual sources tell us nothing of the intervening years between Moses' rescue from the Nile and his adulthood. When we next see him, Moses is fully grown. He witnesses a taskmaster beating a Hebrew slave, kills the Egyptian, and flees to Midian. There he marries Zipporah, daughter of Jethro, and tends his father-in-law's flocks of sheep. Moses lives a comfortable life until the day he encounters the burning bush and Yahweh's call on Mount Sinai (also called Horeb). God orders Moses to go before Pharaoh and demand the release of the Hebrews.

Moses raises objections to this calling. After all, he doesn't know this God's name. What will he tell the Israelites when they ask who has sent him? "Yahweh," God replies, means "I AM WHO I AM, I WILL BE WHO I WILL BE, I CAUSE TO HAPPEN." Moses further objects that he can't speak well and is thus an unsuitable messenger for Yahweh. Not letting him off the hook, God tells him that Aaron, his brother, will assist him and speak for him. "Send someone else!" Moses cries. Angrily, God dismisses Moses' reluctance and reassures him of God's presence and help.

When he returns to Egypt, Moses finds a new pharaoh who not only refuses his request, but responds by oppressing the Hebrews still further. Pharaoh's hardness of heart and the people's brokenness of spirit are two recurring themes in the Exodus narrative. Moses must contend with both.

On one level, the conflict between Yahweh and the gods of Egypt, represented by the king, is a cosmic one. Pharaoh makes fresh promises after each plague to release the Israelites, only to take them back when the danger has passed. With signs and wonders Yahweh prevails and liberates the people. On another level, the conflict persists throughout the history of Israel. They too make continual promises, sincere pledges to uphold the covenant. "All that the LORD has spoken we will do" (Exod. 19:8; 24:3). But when trapped at the edge of the sea (Exod. 14), when hungry in the wilderness (Exod. 16), when left unattended while Moses is with Yahweh on Sinai (Exod. 32), the peoples' hope dissolves and their faith fails. The heart and will of Israel continually conflict with this God of Abraham, Isaac, and Jacob.

At the same time, in spite of Israel's failed attempts at faithfulness, the Exodus event became (and remains) the one moment, the one memory, that bound the people together and to God. *Pesach,* the festival of Passover, was first celebrated in Egypt (Exod. 12) and is still celebrated annually to this day. Whatever the timing or the particulars of their history, the covenant people of Israel understand that *Pesach* does not simply commemorate some past event. Instead, as the Passover ritual states, "In every generation, every person is obligated to see himself as if he went out of Egypt." The one phrase repeated throughout the *Seder* meal, the special ceremonial dinner of *Pesach,* is "Last year we were slaves; this year we are free," For Jews, God's deliverance is relived anew each year: "His lovingkindness has overwhelmed us."

INTO THE WILDERNESS: THE COMING OF THE LAW

As mentioned earlier, the second main section of the Book of Exodus (chapters 19–40) deals with the giving of the Law to Moses on Mount Sinai. Like the Exodus event, the giving of the Law was a defining moment for the band of Israelites wandering in the desert. And here it is helpful to note when the Law is given in the Torah: the first actual law—"the ordinance for the passover" (Exod. 12:43)—appears in the text only after the hymn celebrating God's creation: only after the narrative of God's calling of Abraham, Isaac, and Jacob, and only after the event of God's dramatic deliverance of the people from slavery. The arrangement of the Torah makes clear that the commandments God gives to Israel are ultimately connected to the history of God's activities on behalf of Israel. "What is the meaning of the decrees and the statutes and the ordinances that the LORD our God has commanded you?" asks Deuteronomy 6:20. And the answer Israelite parents are to give their children is: "We were Pharaoh's slaves in Egypt, but the LORD brought us out of Egypt with a mighty hand" (6:21).

Thus, the Law recorded in these chapters from Exodus 20 through Numbers 10 (and repeated in Deuteronomy in the form of sermons delivered by Moses to the second generation out of Egypt) establishes various regulations both for human behavior in relation to other human beings and human behavior in relation to God. The Law covers every arena of community life, from building parapets on the roofs of new houses (Deut. 22:8) to sabbath observances (Deut. 5:12-15).

In these legal texts, scholars have recognized two major types of laws: casuistic and apodictic. Casuistic or case laws consist of two parts. The first part states a condition (If this happens . . .) and the second part the legal consequences (. . . then this will be the punishment). These laws—which we also find in Hammurabi's Code dating from eighteenth century B.C. Babylon—generally concern problems that might arise in agricultural and town life. For example: "If someone's ox hurts the ox of another, so that it dies, then they shall sell the live ox and divide the price of it" (Exod. 21:35).

Apodictic law is represented by the Ten Commandments or Decalogue (Greek for "ten words") first found in Exodus 20:1-21 and repeated in Deuteronomy 5:6-21. Another set of apodictic law is found after the fashioning of the golden calf in Exodus 34:14-26. Apodictic laws are unequivocal statements of the will of God for human behavior. They are cast in the form of commands ("You shall") or prohibitions ("You shall not"). Some scholars think that this form of law is unique to Israel; other Ancient Near Eastern societies certainly had similar sets of laws, but Israel recognized the Decalogue as containing absolute imperatives from God that applied to every member, regardless of social status.

> **Other Ancient Near Eastern societies certainly had similar sets of laws, but Israel recognized the Decalogue as containing absolute imperatives from God that applied to every member, regardless of social status.**

For the Israelites, their Law was not based on an abstract set of rules. It was not an arbitrary legal code forced on Israel. The Law, in fact, all of the Torah, from Genesis through Deuteronomy, was rooted in the covenant established

46

between God and God's people. The commandments that were given to guide the distinctive way of life and faith of Israel were set in the context of the mutual relationship of God's gracious acts and Israel's grateful response. Just as the Torah is always understood within a historical context, the Torah is also understood within a relational context. "Remember this day on which you came out of Egypt, out of the house of slavery, because the LORD brought you out from there by strength of hand" (Exod. 13:3) is just as vital a command-ment for Israel as "you shall love the alien as yourself" (Lev. 19:34). This pow-erful memory of liberation, kept alive in the Exodus story and through the Torah, means that neither neighbor nor sojourner is to be oppressed. As a result, to this day, strangers are invited to join families at the Passover Seder, that freedom may be extended to all.

The journey of Abraham's descendants and the trajectory of the biblical text from Genesis 27 through Deuteronomy 34 move between the land of Egypt and the land of promise, between the covenant of Yahweh and the strug-gles of Israel to stay true to that covenant. The one constant is God. Even as Joseph sits in prison or his brothers contemplate starvation, God's providence is never in doubt. Even as Moses trembles beside the burning bush or quakes before Pharaoh, God's presence is never in question. Even as the Israelites complain in the wilderness or dance before the golden calf, God's promise is never withdrawn. And all along, the principle refrain is "Remember . . ."

INVITATION TO DISCIPLESHIP

The Scriptures we read for this session are some of the most important and memorable in all the Bible. Recall Joseph weeping on the neck of Benjamin after revealing his identity to his stunned brothers: "God sent me before you to preserve for you a remnant on earth . . ." (Gen. 45:7). Recall God addressing Moses out of a burning bush: "Remove the sandals from your feet, for the place on which you are standing is holy ground" (Exod. 3:5). Or Moses standing on the bank of the Nile facing down the great Pharaoh: "The LORD, the God of the Hebrews, sent me to say to you, 'Let my people go . . .'" (Exod. 7:16). Picture Miriam, tambourine in hand, dancing and singing a song (perhaps the oldest text in the Bible) in praise of God's deliverance: "Sing to the LORD, for he has triumphed gloriously; horse and rider he has thrown into the sea" (Exod. 15:21). Imagine hearing Yahweh thunder audibly from the mountain: "You shall have no other gods before me" (Exod. 20:3). Or hearing Moses declare to a second generation of Israelites the sum of their covenant faith: "Hear O Israel, the LORD is our God, the LORD alone. You shall love the LORD your God with all your heart, and with all your soul, and with all your might" (Deut. 6:4-5).

These powerful texts rehearse and celebrate the events that shaped the people of Israel. They are intended to call to mind God's mighty acts of deliverance and command for obedience, as well as God's call for response from those God has chosen and delivered. The meaning of these formational narratives, however, is not locked in a time past. We read, remember, recite, and even sing these words today as our Scripture. A question we might ask ourselves then is, What does Israel's "Exodus faith" mean for us? What deliverance by our God do we celebrate? How might we, like Joseph or Moses, participate in God's ongoing work of liberation in our world today?

FOR REFLECTION

- Read aloud Genesis 50:20. In light of your study this week, how does this verse reflect the theme of the Scriptures you read? How is the voice of the text calling you to respond?

- What are some of the "foundational narratives" or Bible passages that you remember, recite, or sing as your Scripture?

- What does Israel's "Exodus faith" mean for you? What deliverance by God do you celebrate as part of your faith story?

DIGGING DEEPER

Read articles in a Bible dictionary or other resource about the Hyksos Dynasty, the later Egyptian dynasties, Rameses II, Hammurabi (or Hammurapi), and Mount Sinai.

Locate an English translation of the text of Hammurabi's Code and compare it with the material in the Covenant Code found in Exodus 20:22–23:33. Several Web sites provide the complete text of Hammurabi's Code.

Promise and Problem in the Land

Choose this day whom you will serve, whether the gods your ancestors
served in the region beyond the River or the gods of the Amorites in
whose land you are living; but as for me and my household,
we will serve the Lord.

—Joshua 24:15

INTRODUCTION

Our readings this week cover the Israelites' entry into Canaan and the change from a tribal system to a monarchy. Not surprisingly, this period, from roughly 1200 to 1000 B.C., is a time of great transition. Transitional times are by definition unsettling; the books of Joshua and Judges especially reflect this disjointedness and ambivalence. Both books agree that any Canaanite presence is a threat to the covenant, but they are ambiguous with regard to how pervasive that presence actually was. The Book of Joshua describes a campaign of military conquest as the Israelites take control of the Promised Land and attempt to wipe out the Canaanite influence. However, in the Book of Judges, the tribes still struggle on local levels with the native elements and the conquest is far from complete. The Book of First Samuel marks the end of the era of judges with the Israelites' desire for a king. While some parts of the narrative see this desire as a potentially positive one, other parts of the narrative view this desire as a rejection of God's rule and warn that the monarchy will bring no end of trouble. The one consistent perspective in First Samuel is that David is the Lord's anointed, fit to rule and blessed by God.

51

DAILY ASSIGNMENTS

The general perspective of the narratives immediately following the Pentateuch is that establishing their place in the land of promise turns out to be as much of a problem and struggle for Israel as getting there in the first place. As you read through each passage of Scripture this week, keep in mind the following questions: (1) What do you think is the problem with the Canaanite presence in the Promised Land? (2) In what ways is the monarchy a good thing for Israel? (3) In what ways is the monarchy a challenge for Israel?

DAILY PRAYER PSALM: Psalm 119:25-32

DAY ONE: Joshua 1; 2; 6; 24

In what sense is Joshua a worthy successor to Moses? How does his role differ from that of Moses?

move away from Gold —
more idols are described

DAY TWO: Judges 2–4; 6–8   *6 1-18*

What are the positive as well as negative characteristics of Israelite "judges"? What signs of political instability do you find in this period?

• Idol worship
• milk & honey

DAY THREE: 1 Samuel 1–3; 8–12; 15

Note the special role of Samuel as a transitional figure from judgeship to monarchy. How is Israel's first king, Saul, described in the text?

DAY FOUR: 1 Samuel 16–18

What is it about the young David that makes him special? How does the text let you know that he will succeed as king?

God choice — courage —
long Saul

DAY FIVE: 1 Samuel 20; 26; 28; 31

Trace the rise of David and the corresponding decline of Saul. What part of this gripping narrative do you find most interesting? Why?

DAY 6: Commentary

Read the commentary in the participant book.

JOSHUA:
SETTLING IN THE LAND

The Book of Joshua is as much a theological story of Israel's entry into the land of promise as it is an account of how that entry took place. In fact, many scholars suggest that the books of Joshua through Kings were written from an overarching, theological perspective, referred to as the Deuteronomistic History. Informed by Deuteronomy, and perhaps written in the time of King Josiah or during the Babylonian Exile, Joshua through Kings chronicle the rise and fall of God's covenant people in Canaan. Early on the compilers of this material make explicit the connections between Moses and Aaron—representing the roles of leader and priest, first recipients of the Torah, who anticipate entering the Promised Land—and the next generation, led by Joshua and Aaron's son Eleazar, who actually take control of the Promised Land. Just as Moses led the Hebrews out of Egypt by crossing through the Red Sea (or Sea of Reeds), so Joshua leads them into Canaan by crossing through the Jordan River (Josh. 4). Just as Moses celebrated the first Passover with the Hebrew people in Egypt, so Joshua and the Israelites eat the Passover meal outside Jericho (Josh. 5). Just as Moses enacted the covenant based on Torah obedience at an assembly on Mount Sinai, so Joshua renews this covenant at an assembly in Shechem (Josh. 24).

Deuteronomistic History

The Deuteronomistic History is a scholarly designation referring to the material found in the books of Joshua through Second Kings, as well as Deuteronomy 1–4 and 27–30. The general consensus is that these books reveal an overall thematic unity—the call to obedience to Yahweh's covenant—and a similarity in style and language to the Book of Deuteronomy.

Key to the overarching theme of this Deuteronomistic History in general, and the Book of Joshua in particular, is the primary role Yahweh plays in the conquest of Canaan as recorded in Joshua 1–12. According to the text, this God-sanctioned war is swift and miraculous. God fights for the Israelites against all odds and without conventional methods. The ark of the covenant, a gold-overlaid wooden chest that held the tablets of the covenant, was carried by priests in the battlefield. The ark represented God's presence; thus the presence of the ark on the battlefield signified that the battles were led and directed by Yahweh on behalf of Israel. Remarkably, Jericho, the first Canaanite town that Joshua's troops encountered after crossing the Jordan

River from the east, was taken by a shout (Josh. 6:20). The message is clear: the victory is God's, and the enemy, anyone opposed to the God of Israel, is to be utterly destroyed.

This practice of utterly destroying everything in a conquered city is one of the most troubling features of the Book of Joshua. Called *herem* in Hebrew, or "the ban," this practice meant that all Canaanite influence was to be eliminated. All human beings, their animals, possessions, and any booty whatsoever were to be offered up as a great sacrifice to God. From the point of view of the inhabitants (and likely to modern readers), *herem* was ethnic cleansing or religious genocide. Modern scholars debate whether *herem* is to be understood literally or hyperbolically, whether it was a sacrifice or a misunderstanding of God's order. Scholars also point out that the archaeological evidence in support of the annihilation of the Canaanites cities as recorded in Joshua is complex and inconclusive. Nonetheless, readers who focus on the era described in Joshua, as well as in Judges and First Samuel, rightly find this depiction of war and slaughter by God's people in God's name morally repugnant.

Moreover the concept of *herem* raises the difficult question of whether Gentiles, or non-Israelites, are worthy of God's love and care. It was a characteristic of the times that military conquest called for elimination of all foreign influences. But it is important to bear in mind that there was another perspective in the Bible, found as early as the threefold promise to Abraham, with a different outlook on foreigners. According to this view, Israel's role is to benefit other nations: "Through you all the families of the earth will be blessed" (Gen. 12:3; 22:18). Recall that the story of the conquest of Canaan includes the episode of Rahab, a citizen of Jericho, an innkeeper, and a prostitute. She is a Canaanite, a Gentile, and yet she is also a heroine. In Joshua 2, she hides the Israelite spies from the king or chieftain of the town by keeping them safe on her flat rooftop, protecting them from the search party with a bit of deception. According to the text, she has heard of the Israelites and their God. Indeed, Rahab knows—better than the Israelites who often grumble and complain and forget their covenant with Yahweh—that "the LORD has given you the land" (Josh. 2:9). This foreigner inspires the confidence of the spies who return and report to the camp: "Truly the LORD has given all the land into our hands" (2:24).

Again, as troubling as these stories of violence are in Joshua, it is worth remembering that these texts are concerned ultimately with presenting Yahweh as the one God who authorizes and assists in Israel's possession of the land of promise. The land is of utmost theological importance. The land is

God's gift to God's people. But the land is also given only on the condition of Torah obedience. The Scriptures themselves attest to this by framing the conquest narrative on one side by Joshua's commissioning of the people before they cross the Jordan (Josh. 1:7-8) and on the other side by Joshua's challenge to the people at Shechem to choose Yahweh and reject both their ancestral gods and all the gods of Canaan. The people answered, "The LORD our God we will serve, and him we will obey" (Josh. 24:24). Joshua set up a stone as a memorial to the event and a witness to the people's pledge. However the Baals and Astartes, male and female fertility gods of the land, will continue to be powerful and persistent temptations for the Israelites after their settlement in Canaan. The people will turn to the local gods of nature for good crops and good luck. They will relegate Yahweh to one day a week of sabbath observance and give a nod to Yahweh for the history of their deliverance from Egypt. They will be prudent and practical by covering all the bases. Israel has much to learn about this God whom Rahab the foreigner recognizes clearly, as she declares: "The LORD your God is indeed God in heaven above and on earth below" (Josh. 2:11).

JUDGES: LIVING IN THE LAND

At his death, Joshua had not appointed a successor, and the conquest of Canaan was by no means complete (Josh. 13:1-17). Joshua's generation pledged their loyalty to Yahweh, but the next generation "did not know [Yahweh] or the work that he had done for Israel" (see Judg. 2:6-10). The next era, lasting from roughly 1200 to 1030 B.C., is characterized by a loose confederation of disparate tribes. As a confederacy, Israel was dominated by regional interests and foreign oppressors demanding tribute. Times were desperate. The very real problem of living in a land inhabited by other peoples is a recurring theme in the Book of Judges. And beneath that problem is the more crucial theological problem of how failure to obey the Torah threatens Israel's very possession of the land.

During this period, the leaders were known as "judges," or tribal chieftains. With the exception of Deborah and Samuel, the judges had no legal role. They were local military leaders who applied God's judgment to Israel's enemies— in particular the Philistines, who arrived on the Canaanite coastal plain about the same time Joshua led the Israelites across the Jordan River. The Philistines would be Israel's most formidable foe in the period of settlement.

Thirteen leaders are mentioned in the Book of Judges; six only briefly. Very early in the narrative a pattern emerges, beginning with the first judge, Othniel, in Judges 3:1-12. This narrative pattern or cycle is repeated throughout the book and goes like this:

Disobedience: The Israelites turn from Yahweh to worship the local gods.

Defeat: The Lord allows foreign elements (Amorites, Moabites, Canaanites, Midianites, Philistines) to subdue and oppress a tribe or tribes.

Distress: The Israelites cry out to Yahweh, who hears them and raises up a judge.

Deliverer: The judge drives the foreign element out. For as long as the judge is alive, the land is at rest.

Death: But with the judge's death, the people return to their backsliding and forgetful ways; and the cycle begins again.

Throughout this period of the judges, the life of Israel is characterized by oppression, guerrilla warfare, and anarchy, interspersed with brief periods of peace for as long as the judge is alive. When the "spirit of the LORD" descends on a judge, it endows that person with unique military abilities (Judg. 3:10; 6:34; 11:29; 13:25) that cannot be passed down to an heir. What some scholars call the "dark ages of Israel" is evident from the last verse in the book: "In those days there was no king in Israel; all the people did what was right in their own eyes" (21:25). The editors of the Book of Judges clearly felt the need for a faithful king who would lead the people back to Torah obedience, back to God, and finally lead to the elimination of the problems of living in the land of promise.

> **The editors of the book of Judges clearly felt the need for a faithful king who would lead the people back to Torah obedience, back to God, and finally lead to the elimination of the problems of living in the land of promise.**

SAMUEL:
A KING IN THE LAND

The Book of Samuel picks up the story at this point, recounting the rise of kingship. The stories of Israel's first kings are divided into three sections, each based on a major figure. Samuel, the last of the judges, is the subject of 1 Samuel 1–12. Saul, the first of the kings, is the subject of 1 Samuel 13–31. David is introduced and anointed early on in the Saul material, but his official reign begins with the opening of Second Samuel and continues throughout this book. All three figures were pivotal in the development of the Israelite monarchy. The question raised in this material is whether God would again speak through Israel's leaders as in the days of Moses and Joshua. The answer is that a monarchy does not guarantee God's support. The Israelites will not find security in any political system. Torah obedience is what is required.

> **The Israelites will not find security in any political system. Torah obedience is what is required.**

First Samuel opens with a story of barrenness and a miraculous birth. Hannah is unable to conceive. On a pilgrimage to the central sanctuary at Shiloh, she prays for a son and trusts that Yahweh will answer her. Hannah's prayer is answered with the birth of Samuel (whose name means "God heard"), and her celebratory song (1 Sam. 2:1-10) provides the motif for what follows. God brings down the proud; God raises up the lowly. The humble are honored while the mighty are fallen. There is none like God whose ways are unexpected, surprising, unconventional. The theme of reversal will work itself out in the books of Samuel. Although "the word of [Yahweh] was rare in those days; visions were not widespread" (3:1), Yahweh appeared to the young Samuel in the middle of the night as he slept near the ark of the covenant. The message he received was that Eli's family would be removed from office. From then on, the word of Yahweh was revealed to Samuel, and he was recognized by everyone to be a prophet or mouthpiece of God. As Samuel grew, the Lord was with him, letting none of his words fail (3:19).

For a time, Samuel, also called "judge," subdues the Philistines and brings peace to Israel. But recognizing that Samuel will pass on and that there will be no fit successor to lead them, the people approach Samuel with a demand for change. They want a king so they can be "like other nations" (8:5). Samuel is distressed and believes the desire to be like other nations is a rejection of God's rule. Monarchy will bring them a new form of oppression—this time from one of their own. But remarkably, Yahweh instructs Samuel to fulfill their request.

THE EARLY MONARCHY

Samuel now takes on the role of kingmaker with Yahweh's first choice, Saul. In a ceremony involving pouring olive oil over his head, Samuel declares Saul an "anointed one." The Hebrew, rendered "messiah" in English, is merely a title attached to a divinely designated leader in the Hebrew Bible. From the beginning, the text of First Samuel offers a conflicted assessment of Saul. On one hand, he is a tall, handsome man (9:2), a kingly sort. Yet he hides himself among baggage when he is supposed to be crowned (10:22). The spirit of Yahweh comes on him for a time; yet there is a tragic flaw in his character, and the spirit will depart from him. The texts that favor Saul and the monarchy are found in 1 Samuel 9:1–10:16 and 11:1-11. An opposing perspective is found in 1 Samuel 8:1-22; 10:17-27; 11:12–12:25. Both sources agree that the monarchy is not absolute. Both king and people must be subject to God's covenant and its demands.

Nonetheless, the fledgling monarchy begins to take shape—though falteringly at first. Saul starts things off by breaking the rules of holy war, sparing the Amalekite king, Agag, and taking some of the booty. Samuel rebuked him for his disobedience to Yahweh's commands: "Though you are little in your own eyes, are you not the head of the tribes of Israel?" (1 Sam. 15:17). Though Saul repents and asks for forgiveness, Samuel pronounces God's judgment on him: "You have rejected the word of the LORD, and the LORD has rejected you from being king over Israel" (1 Sam. 15:26). Although Saul remained in office until his death, Samuel anoints another king to take his place.

This newly appointed successor to Saul is David, the youngest son of Jesse, who comes from the small village of Bethlehem. Such humble origins make David an unlikely candidate for leadership. However, David's character is assessed positively from the beginning. Yahweh knew David's heart (1 Sam. 16:7). The shepherd boy overturns the Philistine giant, Goliath, and arrives at the king's court to play the lyre and soothe Saul's troubled soul. David befriends Saul's son Jonathan and marries Saul's daughter, Michal (ch. 18). He wins the hearts of all Israel with his "Robin Hood" tactics against the Philistines.

While David's star is on the rise, Saul's is on the decline. Saul's jealousy and paranoia cause him to pursue David and turn on anyone who helped him, including his own son (1 Sam. 20:33). But when David has the opportunity to stop him and put an end to Saul's pursuit, he twice declares that he will not raise a hand against Saul (24:6; 26:11). Saul's obsession with eliminating David is a tragic tale: no matter how Saul tries, David's success is unstoppable.

And the Book of First Samuel closes with Saul's final battle. Mortally wounded by a Philistine, Saul falls on his own sword, and his sons die in battle. It is now time for new leadership. David will be anointed king. The people now living in the land God had given them now have a king God has given them. But just as the gift of land came with warnings and challenges, so too comes the gift of a king. The call of Joshua to "choose this day whom you will serve" will con-tinue to be the greatest challenge for the people—and now their kings.

INVITATION TO DISCIPLESHIP

What God asks the Israelites to do is trust in God's faithful care, in spite of appearances to the contrary, and obey God's ordering of their lives, in spite of the difficulties it may entail. In the eyes of this band of formerly wandering, ex-slaves from Egypt, the Canaanites seemingly have the military advantage in war, protected by walled cities and possessing bigger armies. The Canaanites are well-established in the land with cultural practices and polytheistic religious beliefs that are at odds with Israel's way of life and worship of Yahweh. It is not hard to see parallels with our contemporary situation. Choosing to trust in God's faithful care is not so difficult when times are joyous and carefree. But what about when trouble comes? Choosing to worship on Sundays when we are feeling good and the family is there in the pew is not such a challenge. But what about the rest of our week? Choosing to obey God's ordering of our way of life seems manageable in the quiet of our morning prayers. But what happens when career, school, relationships, possessions, finances, sports, the media, all start clamoring for our attention?

"Choose this day whom you will serve." Our key verse implies two things: (1) choices are ours to make, and (2) we will inevitably find something or someone to serve. Choices are real and ever before us. Recall the many choices Israel had to make in this week's readings. How did Israel's choices (or the choices of Israel's leaders) affect their existence in the land of promise? What were the consequences when something other than obedience to Yahweh was chosen? Like the people of Israel, we are beings with hearts and wills that are free, within limits, to choose. This is what it means to be human. Being human also means that we are made to serve. Being human means we submit our wills to something. That something might be a quest for power and success. Or we might simply submit ourselves to fate or circumstances. Whether we do so consciously or unconsciously, we are always choosing to serve something. And we are always reaping the consequences of those choices.

"Choose this day. . . ." What will it be? What will it take for you to choose this day—and every day—to trust in God's faithful care?

FOR REFLECTION

• Read aloud Joshua 24:15. In light of your study this week, how does this verse reflect the theme of the Scriptures you read? How is the voice of the text calling you to respond?

• How would you describe Israel's land of promise? How did Israel's choices affect their existence in their land of promise? How would you describe your "land of promise"? How have your choices affected the way you live in your "land of promise"?

• What does it take for you to choose this day—and every day—to trust in God's faithful care?

DIGGING DEEPER

Read articles in a Bible dictionary or other resource about some of the cities mentioned in the conquest narratives of Joshua—Jericho, Ai, Bethel, Hazor.

Read about the Philistines and their way of life.

Research the religious beliefs and practices of the Canaanites by reading about Ras Shamra and the tablets discovered there. (See *Understanding the Old Testament*, Anderson, pp. 169–171.

Israel Has a King

Your house and your kingdom shall be made sure forever before me;
your throne shall be established forever.

—*2 Samuel 7:16*

INTRODUCTION

By the end of the Book of Judges, it appears that the people of Israel are in trouble. "In those days there was no king in Israel; all the people did what was right in their own eyes" (Judg. 21:25). The tribal confederacy described in First Samuel is fractious and the house of Eli is corrupt. In addition, the threat of wholesale takeover by the powerful Philistines with their superior iron weapons was very real. There was clearly a need for leadership. However, when the people petitioned Samuel for a king, his response was reluctant, cautioning them to be careful what they wish for (1 Sam. 8). Throughout the books of Samuel, this tension persists: in spite of the apparent need for some new governance model, the establishment of kingship in Israel bodes both potential and peril.

At first Samuel's warning seems well founded. Israel's first king, Saul, is a failure, a tragic figure. But then comes David. The reign of this humble shepherd boy inaugurates a golden age in Israel. Under David, Israel was at last united in its place among the other nations and in its worship of Yahweh. Future kings would be evaluated in light of his achievements. Sadly none will measure up.

DAILY ASSIGNMENTS

In the ancient world, portraits of the powerful were often painted in either black or white terms. The material in Second Samuel offers a complex portrait of David as both a public figure and a private individual who is finally human, just like us. David's character is great and deeply flawed. His heart is magnanimous and manipulative. His story, like ours, is not an easy one to tell. Reading Second Samuel closely invites us to read our own lives—our motives, our words and actions—in new ways. As you read, keep in mind the following questions: (1) How does this narrative portray King David? (2) Why do you think David is remembered as the ideal king?

DAILY PRAYER PSALM: Psalm 111

DAY ONE: 2 Samuel 1–2; 5–6

Note the particularly vivid details of this court history. Where do you see political lines drawn between David's supporters and supporters of Saul's family?

776
pg 777

DAY TWO: 2 Samuel 7

In what ways do you interpret the Davidic covenant delivered by the prophet Nathan?

Do all that is in your heart for the Lord
Build me a house of cedar
rest from your enemies

DAY THREE: 2 Samuel 11–12

What does the episode with Bathsheba tell you about David? About God's judgment on David and his dynasty?

· fell to temptation
· he was not pleased

DAY FOUR: 2 Samuel 13; 15:1–19:8

· pg 80

Note Absalom's drive for power and David's blind eye toward his son.

· rent = mean

DAY FIVE: 2 Samuel 22:1–23:7; Psalms 18; 22; 23: 51; 89

What do these psalms tell you about David's heart?

· elated / depression
· mood swings   journey sides
·   leadership
· blind eye   character

DAY 6: Commentary

Read the commentary in the participant book.

PORTRAIT OF THE KING

David had led the life of an outlaw, an Israelite "Robin Hood" with his band of merry men, while Saul was still alive. He had allied himself with the Philistine king, Achish, to ensure the safety of his retinue of six hundred men and two wives. During the time he was under Achish's protection, David pillaged neighboring Philistine towns and won supporters back home. It is under these conditions that he receives word of Saul's and Jonathan's death in the opening chapter of Second Samuel.

David's eulogy (2 Sam. 1:19-27) is one of the most moving in biblical poetry. The verses attest to his admiration for Saul and his devotion to Jonathan, Saul's son. "I am distressed for you, my brother Jonathan; greatly beloved were you to me" (1:26). His grief is evident and real.

Yet David is a strategist. He will benefit from the upheaval caused by the death of Saul and his sons. There is a dissent among the tribes, dividing the northern tribes, supporting Saul, from the southern tribe of Judah, David's home. Immediately after the eulogy, David goes to Hebron where he is anointed king over Judah. Saul's fourth and only remaining son, Ishbaal, had been proclaimed king in the North by Abner, Saul's commander-in-chief.

Over the next seven years, what remains of the house of Saul crumbles. Both Ishbaal and Abner are assassinated. David is not directly involved in these murders and publicly mourns their deaths; yet the reader knows that David will benefit from the power vacuum in the North. The elders of Israel (the northern tribes) approach him with an offer to be king (2 Sam. 5:3), and David graciously accepts. He is only thirty years old. All serious rivals have been dispatched. For the next thirty-three years, David will be king over North and South. It is a fragile unity inspired by a charismatic ruler.

He leads troops to capture the town of Jebus, also in Judah, moving the capital from Hebron and establishing this new capital as Jerusalem, "the city of David." He immediately fetches the ark of the covenant and brings it to the city for permanent dwelling there. It is a scene of sheer joy and exuberance (2 Sam. 6). David dances before the ark half-clad, in ecstasy, and wild abandon. Michal, Saul's daughter and one of David's wives, despises him for this unseemly behavior. But nothing can temper his enthusiasm; his only concern is the celebration of the ark's homecoming. We see here the heart God knew and loved. It is time to dance with the Lord, to sing and shout, to celebrate. This is not the time for strategy and calculated moves. This portrait of David abides in the memory of Israel.

TROUBLE AT HOME

With the consolidation of the kingdom and the establishment of a capital city, the golden age of Israel begins. Second Samuel 8:15 summarizes the rightness and justice of David's reign: "So David reigned over all Israel; and David administered justice and equity to all his people." God protects both David and the fledgling nation. There is peace at home, and God promises that the house of David will continue into the future (2 Sam. 7). Politically and publicly, David is everything the people could want.

David's personal life, however, is another thing. In the episode with Bathsheba, David is described as a ruthless and calculating individual (2 Sam. 11). The narrative in 2 Samuel 9–20 (and in 1 Kings 1–2) is told with such detail that scholars suspect the source was an eyewitness to the scandal and intrigue. This is no airbrushed biography. This story depicts a man who takes what he wants, because he has the power, and covers his tracks with deception and bloodshed.

> **Politically and publicly, David is everything the people could want. David's personal life, however, is another thing.**

David coveted and used Bathsheba. When she sends him word that she is pregnant, David quickly orders her husband, Uriah, home. David thinks he can wash his hands of the trouble he has caused with a paternity scheme. But his plans are frustrated. Uriah refuses to sleep with his wife while his soldiers were still on the battlefield, adhering to the ancient custom of sexual abstinence among soldiers during war. So David sends the loyal Uriah to the front. In a chilling stroke, we learn that Uriah carries his own death warrant to the commander, Joab. When David receives word of the suicide mission, he shows no regard for the casualties who fell in battle. After all, he learns with satisfaction that, "your servant Uriah the Hittite is dead also" (2 Sam. 11:24).

THUS SAYS THE LORD

David is capable of cool-headed strategy as well as impulsive action. One is not better than the other; both can be abused and misused. As he dances before the Lord in Jerusalem, or as he mourns the death of his friend, Jonathan, we feel his heart is full to bursting. We rejoice in his magnanimity, his bigheartedness. He inspires love and loyalty from his fellow Israelites. Dissident voices are silenced, however, by assassinations and untimely deaths. Although his commander, Joab, takes care of the dirty work, we know that David's hands are not clean.

The need for dependence on God rather than fulfillment of one's immediate desires is a thread that carries through all of Second Samuel. The narrative shows the importance of obedience to the Torah in contrast to a king's impulse to put his own desires above the law. Crucial to this history is the prophet Nathan, who addresses David's actions and makes known "the word of the LORD."

The Ancient Near Eastern model of governance made the king creator of law and put the king above the law. But in Israel covenantal values collided with kingly power.

Nathan appears out of nowhere. All we know is that he is a *nabi*, spokesperson, and that he has access to the court whenever he pleases. Importantly for Israel, along with the role of king came the role of prophet. And while such a role is essential for the story of Israel from this point on, much of the rest of the Old Testament will show that the relationship between prophet and king is always problematic. King Ahab will call Elijah a "troubler of Israel" (1 Kings 18:17) and will say of another *nabi*: "I hate him, for he never prophesies anything favorable about me" (1 Kings 22:8). It is to David's credit that Nathan, the truth-teller, is allowed a presence in the royal household.

The Ancient Near Eastern model of governance made the king creator of law and put the king above the law. But in Israel covenantal values collided with kingly power. The prophet, God's spokesperson, challenges this royal prerogative. He reminds both ruler and nation that God's ways are not the ways of the power-driven world.

But first Nathan tells a parable (2 Sam. 12:1-4). Nathan describes a poor man who has one ewe lamb, which is near and dear to him, like a child. His rich neighbor, who possesses many flocks, takes the one lamb away and slaughters it. The rich man does so simply because it is convenient and because he can.

The parable Nathan delivers gives David the opportunity to see what has truly happened. The prophet holds up a mirror, and David sees his true reflection at last. Then Nathan moves into direct confrontation: "Thus says the LORD." The Lord has given David everything. What David took to be his achievements and his divine right were not his to claim. David's actions will have consequences. And the consequences will work themselves out in the next generation as David's sons vie for succession to the throne.

Nathan delivers the chilling truth: "Thus says the LORD: I will raise up trouble against you from within your own house" (2 Sam. 12:11). As David has destroyed the family of Uriah, so his own family will be destroyed. The sins of David's private life would become public in the lives of his children. Bathsheba's baby takes sick and dies. Amnon, David's first-born son, rapes Tamar the sister of Absalom, David's third-born. Absalom later murders Amnon, leads a revolt against his father, and briefly takes control of Jerusalem. His very own son does before all Israel what David did secretly (2 Sam. 16:22). David, the brave shepherd boy, the mighty king, is a miserable failure as husband and father.

THE DAVIDIC COVENANT

More even than Saul, David deserves to be removed from the throne. But the kingdom is not taken from him as it was from Saul. Why?

We must go back to 2 Samuel 7 and set the context. There we find another meeting of prophet and king. While David is making plans to build a temple, Nathan arrives unexpectedly. "Thus says the LORD," he begins. David will not be the one to build a house for God. Then Nathan delivers an oracle that is as astounding as it is far-reaching. The Lord promises to build a house for David. And as our key verse states: "Your house and your kingdom shall be made sure forever before me; your throne shall be established forever" (2 Sam. 7:16). God's promise is sure.

This passage in Second Samuel, known as the Davidic covenant, turns on the multiple meanings of the word house (Hebrew *bayit*). In reference to David's building plan, *bayit* means God's house, the Jerusalem Temple that David's son Solomon will build. In reference to God's future actions, David's *bayit* is also his dynasty, the "house of David." His house will be established forever. What this promise means then, according to the Deuteronomistic historians, is that there would always be a land of Israel, with a capital city, Jerusalem, from which this descendant of David would rule. This "royal theology" or belief in the legitimacy and promise of God's anointed leaders would continue even after the collapse of the monarchy, living on in the messianic expectation of a future deliverer who would reign over God's people from Zion, the city of David. If indeed this material was compiled by the community in exile, then such a promise must have surely sustained those who feared the line of Davidic kings had met its end at the hands of the Babylonians.

"Is not my house like this with God? / For he has made with me an ever-lasting covenant, / ordered in all things and secure" (2 Sam. 23:5), David sings. According to the text, this is David's final word, a hymn praising Yahweh for delivering him and delighting in him. He has enjoyed God's steadfast love. God is the rock of his salvation. David's last psalm looks back on his reign and God's covenant. Notice what he emphasizes in both hymns: justice is the foundation of true God's kingdom; one who rules justly is what God requires. David also knows his success exists only by virtue of God's promises. The everlasting covenant is sure. Exactly how and when God will fulfill the covenant remains an open-ended question.

DAVID, THE PSALMIST

It is significant that David's last word is a psalm of praise. One of the other aspects of the Bible's portrait of David is his authorship of many of the psalms collected in Israel's hymnbook for use in worship. Almost half of the psalms have headings that associate them with David. However "A psalm of David" can be translated in a variety of ways: "dedicated to David," "belonging to David," "concerning David." While tradition ascribes many psalms to him, authorship is not known with certainty.

"This God—his way is perfect; / the promise of the LORD proves true; / he is a shield for all who take refuge in him" (Ps. 18:30). The Hebrew *tamim*, translated here as "perfect," carries the sense of completeness, wholeness., entireness. The psalmist uses the same word two verses later to refer to himself: God makes my way *tamim* (18:32). Clearly any notions of "perfect," meaning "faultless, without flaw," do not pertain to David, or the psalmist—or to us. We see in David's story the meeting of God's ways with the wildly successful, yet conflicted and troubled ways of a king. *Tamim* is fully realized in God's ways. But even for God's anointed, David, as well as for us, *tamim* is a work in progress, a movement with God toward wholeness, toward the time when all of God's people are at last complete.

Psalms in Jewish Liturgy

According to Jewish tradition, specific psalms may be recited on each day of the week.

Sunday	= Psalm 24
Monday	= Psalm 48
Tuesday	= Psalm 82
Wednesday	= Psalm 94
Thursday	= Psalm 81
Friday	= Psalm 93
Saturday	= Psalm 92

INVITATION TO DISCIPLESHIP

As we read Second Samuel, we are invited to read our own lives and motivations in new ways. As we have seen, the narrative traditions that tell the story of Israel's transition from a tribal confederacy to a monarchy were concerned with more than simply recounting historical events. They were also concerned with revealing theological meaning. The text dares to tell the truth about how risky becoming "like other nations" can be. Cultural accommodation turns out to have dire consequences for a people called by God to live distinct from other cultures. The text dares to tell the truth about earthly kingship. Sometimes it works and sometimes it doesn't; but in either case, the problem for Israel is always how to avoid allowing devotion to the king to eclipse devotion to Yahweh. And the text dares to tell the truth about David. The great unifier of Israel could not keep his own family from breaking apart.

We too are challenged to tell the truth about ourselves. Hopefully, as we read the Scriptures this week, we thought about the breach between our own actions and words. We have experienced the heart at its best and at its darkest. These texts invite us to develop an imagination that understands a people struggling to be faithful to God but also to make a life for themselves among people not faithful to their God. These texts ask us to pay attention to David's complexities and ambiguities. In doing so, we are invited to make sense of our own lives, to find what orders and completes us and to examine our own mixed motives and tenuous loyalties.

And don't forget the role of the *nabi* or God's spokesperson. As Nathan did in 2 Samuel 7, the *nabi* brings the message of promise, the good news of God's eternal support for the house of David. But Nathan also holds up a mirror to David, allowing him to see himself as he really is. There are truth-tellers in the biblical story, and there are truth-tellers in our own lives as well. As David made a place in his court for Nathan, we also need to open ourselves to voices we would rather tune out because they make us uncomfortable. We need to attend to people who may appear unlikely spokespersons. Their role is crucial: For without such people, truths about God and about ourselves might not be heard otherwise.

FOR REFLECTION

• Read aloud 2 Samuel 7:16. In light of your study this week, how does this verse reflect the theme of the Scriptures you read? How is the voice of the text calling you to respond?

• When has your allegience to or desire for something not aligned with God's purposes gotten you into trouble?

• Who are the "Nathans" in your life, and how do they hold you accountable in your faith? When have you had to play the role of Nathan to someone? What was the outcome?

DIGGING DEEPER

Read descriptions of the following in a Bible dictionary: the Jebusites, Jerusalem, Kidron, and Gihon.

On a map of the Ancient Near East (see the *Oxford Bible Atlas*, pp. 65, 71, 75), compare the size of David's kingdom with the size of the kingdoms of Assyria, Babylon, and Egypt.

Consider the reasons land has such cultural, physical, and theological significance for Israel.

Division and the Rise of Prophecy

What does the Lord require of you / but to do justice, and to love kindness, / and to walk humbly with your God?

—Micah 6:8

INTRODUCTION

When he was about to die, David counseled his son Solomon: "Be strong, be courageous, and keep the charge of the LORD your God, walking in his ways and keeping his statutes, his commandments, his ordinances, and his testimonies, as it is written in the law of Moses, so that you may prosper in all that you do and wherever you turn" (1 Kings 2:2-3). This advice comes at an auspicious time. The kingdom is united and David's legacy is assured by the covenant of 2 Samuel 7. Two centuries later, however, the landscape has changed. The one United Monarchy is now divided between the ten tribes of Israel in the north and the lone tribe of Judah in the south. To the east, Assyria is on the rise. At home, in both Israel and Judah, there is a false sense of security and a complacent attitude toward idolatry. With alarm, the prophets see the reality of impending doom. What has happened? Why the shift from the colorful days of the early monarchy to the stark black-and-white images painted by the prophets? In the words of 1 Kings 9:9, it is "because they have forsaken the LORD their God, who brought their ancestors out of the land of Egypt, and embraced other gods, worshiping them and serving them. . . ." Intended here as a warning, we can hardly help but hear these words telling the truth that will soon come to pass.

DAILY ASSIGNMENTS

We see in this week's readings the dissolution of David's counsel along with the division of the kingdom. And as the kings of both the North and the South descend deeper into idolatry, leading the people into grave danger, the prophet ascends to prominence with a word from the Lord. Now the prophetic voice must echo, more urgently than ever, King David's final words. Unfortunately, the tension between David's advice to Solomon the son and Yahweh's warning to Solomon the king is clear: the Israelites' desire to become "like other nations" has undercut their resolve to "walk before me [God] in faithfulness."

As you read this week, keep in mind the following questions: (1) What are the dangers of the monarchy for Israel? (2) How do the prophets relate to the political and religious establishments of their time? (3) What hopes do the prophets envision for the future?

DAILY PRAYER PSALM: Psalm 82

DAY ONE: 1 Kings 2:1-4; 3; 5–6; 8–9:9

After reading these passages, what do you understand to be the "wisdom of Solomon"? Why do you think so much attention is paid to the building of the Temple?

DAY TWO: 1 Kings 10–12

Note that Solomon's death is almost immediately followed by the division of the kingdom. Why do you think Jeroboam was successful with his *coup d'etat*? How did Rehoboam, Solomon's son, act unwisely?

DAY THREE: 1 Kings 17–19; 21

Elijah is a prophet best known for his deeds rather than his words. Think about what message his miracles in chapter 17 and his showdown with the Baal prophets in chapter 18 send to Israel. What does the episode of Naboth's vineyard tell you about the monarchy at this time?

DAY FOUR: Amos 3; 5; 7; Hosea 1–3; 5:1–6:6; 11

Amos condemns and frightens in order to provoke change. What judgments does he deliver? Hosea adds a message of hope. How does he use the metaphor of marriage in his message? What does God say about plans for the future?

DAY 5: Micah 3–4; 6; Isaiah 5–6; 9; 11

List as many indictments of the privileged and the rulers that you can find in Micah and Isaiah. Then sketch out (in words or pictures) the key images of the future messianic age, envisioned by these prophets.

DAY SIX: Commentary

Read the commentary in the participant book.

KING SOLOMON
IN ALL HIS GLORY

The seeds of his kingdom's ruin were sown soon after David's death. David died without naming an heir. As a younger son, Solomon's accession was plotted by his mother, Bathsheba; the priest, Zadok; the prophet, Nathan; and the commander, Benaiah. Pitted against this powerful bloc was Adonijah, David's eldest son, supported by the priest, Abiathar, and Joab, David's old general. By the end of 1 Kings 2, Adonijah and his party have all been executed. Remember Nathan's words to David after the death of Uriah: "The sword shall never depart from your house" (2 Sam. 12:10). With all rivals eliminated, court intrigue is suspended and Solomon's reign is secured. For the time being.

Solomon's Temple

Completed about 53 B.C., this glory of Solomon's reign was destroyed by the Babylonians in 587 B.C., rebuilt and rededicated by the returning exiles in 516 B.C., and enlarged by Herod in 20 B.C. only to be destroyed again in A.D. 70.

Today in Jerusalem, the Western Wall contains the only remnants of Herod's Temple expansion. Solomon's great achievement has survivied only as a description in the Bible.

While the completion of the Temple was arguably his greatest achievement, Solomon is most remembered for a dream and a prayer. The dream occurred early his reign, when the Lord appeared to Solomon in his sleep and asked him what he desired. Solomon asks not for strength and power, but for a discerning mind to wisely lead the people (1 Kings 3:9). He wished to govern as God's servant. The Hebrew for what he requested is "a listening heart."

The prayer occurs later at the dedication of the Temple in Jerusalem, a time for self-congratulation and for basking in the nation's admiration. Surprisingly, Solomon publicly prays: "Even heaven and the highest heaven cannot contain you, much less this house that I have built!" (1 Kings 8:27). Solomon in his wisdom knows God is not limited to a particular people or place. Recognizing that God is not contained in the Temple, Solomon nevertheless remembers that God said, "My name shall be there," so that the Temple will be a place that meets human needs and provides people with a time and space for worship.

We may tend to remember Solomon selectively, for his wisdom and understanding; but the text will not allow that. There is ample evidence of both the use and abuse of wisdom in Solomon's policies. Ignoring tribal boundaries, Solomon set up twelve administrative districts in Israel for taxation purposes.

He contracted with Hiram of Tyre to supply materials and builders for the Temple project and an expensive royal palace complex. The money and the labor force came from the Israelites, whose conscription in the building projects was not unlike Pharaoh's enslavement of the Hebrews two centuries earlier. Both the Temple and the king's palace were opulent. Gold overlay abounded everywhere, and at a price. While the Deuteronomistic historian places blame on Solomon's many foreign wives, these women were really political alliances. Nonetheless, one thousand wives requiring expensive upkeep no doubt further burdened national resources. Dissatisfaction grew to the point that, with Solomon's death, the cry went out: "To your tents, O Israel! Look now to your own house, O David" (1 Kings 12:16). Jeroboam leads the revolt in the North while Solomon's sorry son, Rehoboam, is left with Judah in the South. The year is 922 B.C. The division of David's briefly unified kingdom is permanent. The tension between "be strong" and "walk before God" collapses, and with it the glories of Solomon's reign.

THE PROPHET ELIJAH

Beginning with Jeroboam, the kings of Israel (the Northern Kingdom) are condemned for two reasons. They maintained altars with hired priests at Dan and Bethel in direct competition with centralized worship in Jerusalem. Worse, they kept the golden calves that Jeroboam set up, like Aaron had done in the fiasco at Mount Sinai (Exod. 32). One of these northern kings, Ahab, and the prophet who condemns him, Elijah, are the subject of a cycle of stories in I Kings 17–2 Kings 2.

Like Solomon's marriages, Ahab's marriage to Jezebel was made to seal a foreign alliance. She was a zealot who supported upwards of a thousand prophets of Baal and Asherah, male and female deities, in the court at Samaria. Ruthless in her religious fundamentalism and accompanying power politics, Jezebel slaughtered any challenger. She was accustomed to having her way. Elijah, the lone prophet of Yahweh, comes out of nowhere and issues a bold call for change.

First, Elijah declares that the Lord has sent a drought in the land. Baal, also called "the Rider on the Clouds," was the god of fertility who brought the rains. The question posed by Elijah's prediction is: Who is really in control here? If it is Baal, the Israelites could simply bow down before him, practice magic, and live the materialistic life of serving gods of their own making. If, however, Yahweh is in charge, they would have to live by the ethical and moral standards of the Torah. The drought serves as notice that a choice must be made.

The drought persists for three years. The issue finally comes to a head with a dramatic encounter on Mount Carmel between the lone prophet of Yahweh and 450 prophets of Baal. Elijah calls for a contest and sets the conditions, giving every possible advantage to the opposition. The narrator tells the story with delight. The Baal prophets make frantic and lengthy efforts to send down fire on the altar. Elijah sarcastically suggests that their god has wandered off, perhaps to take a nap. He then utters a simple and elegant prayer, which is immediately answered. Fire consumes the altar and the dazzled Israelites proclaim in one voice, "The LORD indeed is God" (1 Kings 18:39). The miracle is huge, and the response is proportionate. Shortly after, the drought ends. Elijah stands at the pinnacle of his prophetic career.

PROPHETS OF THE EIGHTH CENTURY

Elijah and his successor, Elisha, both prophets of ninth-century Israel, are known less for their words than for their actions. A century later, prophets were called who are remembered for their oracles and whose names are attached to books. For example, Amos and Hosea were active in the Northern Kingdom, Isaiah and Micah in the Southern Kingdom. Their messages were collected and preserved in poetic form, each with a unique emphasis, yet sharing the power of the spoken word that always begins, "Thus says the LORD."

> **The dictionary definition of *prophecy* is "a prediction of the future." This popular notion is not the concern of biblical prophets. Their most basic concern was with present behaviors; with the social, political, and religious climate; and with God's demands of justice and covenantal commitment.**

The dictionary definition of *prophecy* is "a prediction of the future." This popular notion is not the concern of biblical prophets. Their most basic concern was with present behaviors; with the social, political, and religious climate; and with God's demands of justice and covenantal commitment. A true prophet confronts an audience and lays bare what God sees. The favorite tense of biblical prophecy is the present.

A prophet is called in times of crisis. The Divided Kingdom was threatened by the external danger of an aggressor, Assyria, and from the hidden internal danger of spiritual complacency and idolatry. The people need to wake up, to see clearly, and thereby to avert disaster. Oracles of judgment and future disaster are contingent on the people's response in the present. The future is not set in stone. Angry warnings are calls for change. Indeed, the anger of God preserved in the prophetic writings reveals a God who is moved by what people do. It is a sign that God's relationship to the people is taken seriously. "I hate, I despise your festivals" (Amos 5:21). These are not the words of an indifferent judge who metes out an icy punishment. The prophets show us the pain and anger of the One whose heart's desires are thwarted by our rebelliousness and disobedience.

Amos is the earliest of these prophets. His message is dated around 760 to 750 B.C. We know from 7:14 that he was a "dresser of sycamore trees," a migrant worker from a little town in Judea called Tekoa, and that he was sent by God to deliver a message to Israel in the north. Although there were professional prophets in the capital city of Samaria, Amos was distanced from them in every way possible. Court prophets spoke as a collective body and gave good news to those in power by whom they were paid. Amos traveled alone, was beholden to no one, and had virtually no good news to give.

Amos saw the complacency and false piety of the people on one hand and the inevitable judgment of God on the other. Formal religious rites were empty, he declared, because what God demands is that "justice roll down like waters / and righteousness like an everflowing stream" (Amos 5:24). God had always applied these standards in God's dealings with Israel. Amos forcefully applied these same standards to how people dealt with one another. The Mosaic covenant bound Israel to Yahweh in a special way. To be chosen, however, did not exempt one from responsibilities to each another. Quite the opposite: "You only have I known / of all the families of the earth; / therefore I will punish you / for all your iniquities" (3:2). Placed alongside the true vertical of justice, Israel is tilted and out of plumb (7:7-9). The kingdom is about to implode, to crash in on itself, along with its religious leaders, court prophets, and acquisitive merchants.

Hosea continues with Amos's theme of judgment in the Northern Kingdom, which fell to Assyria in 721 B.C. The ten tribes were scattered throughout the vast Assyrian Empire in a sort of fruitbasket turnover. Foreigners were brought in to take their place, people who would be later known as Samaritans. His personal story is a tragic one, set up to mirror the very heart of God. Hosea married a woman who was unfaithful; their children were probably not his own. She left him to lead the life of a prostitute, just as Israel has gone after the Baals and left Yahweh for other lovers. "Their deeds do not permit them / to return to their God. / For the spirit of whoredom is within them, / and they do not know the LORD" (Hos. 5:4).

What Hosea added to Amos's dire picture of doom was a note of grace and renewal. Yahweh instructs Hosea to go and buy Gomer back, to redeem her for a price, and to take her back home. There will be a return, a restoration. There will come a time when a new covenant will be made. Israel will again call God "my husband" (Hos. 2:16) in a marriage that is sure, steady, and hard won. Yahweh's steadfast love will not cease. In Hosea 11, the metaphor shifts from marital to parental love. Israel was the child whom the parent led "with cords of human kindness, / with bands of love" (11:4). Yahweh literally hugged the toddler out of Egypt, lifted the infant to God's cheek, bent down and fed the child. The Lord will not—cannot—give them up (11:8).

> **Yahweh literally hugged the toddler out of Egypt, lifted the infant to God's cheek, bent down and fed the child. The Lord will not—cannot—give them up.**

In spite of these prophets' warnings, Judah managed to hold its ground against Assyria for a time. But as members of the sole remaining tribe, Judeans (later Jews) of the eighth-century B.C. believed the holy mount in the capital city, and by extension the Southern Kingdom itself, would be immune from disaster (Mic. 3:11). Isaiah of Jerusalem, whose oracles are collected in our present Isaiah 1–39, and the rural southerner, Micah, declared otherwise. Echoing Amos and Hosea, both oppose the ritualistic righteousness of the pious. Both note how mere religious practice replaces moral and ethical concerns. Both use vivid images: the ruling parties cannibalize the people (Mic. 3:1-3; Isa. 9:11-12); they build Zion with blood (Mic. 3:10). Judah is a wild vineyard that will be trampled down (Isa. 5:5). The axe will fall, and only a remnant will remain.

Yes, proclaimed the prophets, a remnant will remain (Isa. 6:13; 11:16). Both Isaiah and Micah envision a coming age of *shalom*, peace, that is tied to the Davidic covenant but transcends the traditional understanding of it. At some future time, the Lord will raise up a ruler who walks in God's ways with justice and righteousness (Isa. 9:7). The prophetic emphasis shifts from the messianic king to the messianic kingdom, from the house of David to the dream of God, a vision in which "the wolf shall live with the lamb, / the leopard shall lie down with the kid, / the calf and the lion and the fatling together, / and a little child shall lead them" (Isa 11:6). No longer will people study war; instead the nations will stream to Zion to learn God's ways (Mic. 4:1-3). God's dream is of an age of true *shalom*, established and upheld by righteousness and characterized by the love of God and love of the neighbor. God's dream, yet to be realized, will soon be all this remnant of Israel will take with them into exile.

INVITATION TO DISCIPLESHIP

Solomon finally opted for the politics of power rather than the wisdom of the heart. The kings that followed him opted for more of the same, leading Israel to accept widespread cultural accommodation and religious idolatry as a way of life in direct opposition to the way of the covenant. Not surprisingly, the prophets demanded a shift from this status quo of complacency and false piety back to the standards of worship and justice and righteousness commanded by the Torah. Our key verse defines the essence of Torah faith: "What does the LORD require of you / but to do justice, and to love kindness, / and to walk humbly with your God?" (Mic. 6:8). These are not impossible demands. Humans are both required and able to do these very things.

"Be strong, be courageous, and keep the charge of the LORD your God, walking in his ways. . . " (1 Kings 2:2). These words of David presented Solomon—and now present us—with a central challenge: if strength and self-sufficiency are our goals, then we will look for any gods (Baals) we can manipulate and any false prophets who can comfort us. We will construct a world in which we are powerful and sure. We will construe God's promises through a theology of our own making, complete with Temple worship that keeps us safe, and with a confidence that blinds us to our own idolatry.

Like Israel in this week's readings, we live in a culture with other people who worship other gods and who live by other rules. The dangers of complacency and choosing to follow the other gods are as real today as they were in the eighth and ninth centuries. With that in mind, we would do well to ask again what it means to be strong and courageous and to walk in the ways of God. According to Solomon, that means genuinely asking God for a discerning heart. According to Amos or Micah, that means acting justly, loving kindness, and seeking good and not evil. And according to Isaiah, that means walking, not alone, but into the dream of God, looking for the day when the wolf and the lamb can truly live together.

FOR REFLECTION

• Read aloud Micah 6:8. In light of your study this week, how does this verse reflect the theme of the Scriptures you read? How is the voice of the text calling you to respond?

• In what ways are the dangers of complacency and choosing to follow other gods real today?

• What persons speak with a prophetic voice in our day, and what is their message?

DIGGING DEEPER

Read articles in a Bible dictionary or other resource about the Assyrian Empire, Solomon's Temple, high places, Shalmaneser III, Jehu, Sennacherib, Lachish, and Hezekiah.

Locate a diagram or illustration of Solomon's Temple to get a sense of its grandeur and the tragedy of its destruction for Israel.

Exile and Response

How could we sing the LORD's song / in a foreign land?

—*Psalm 137:4*

INTRODUCTION

Home. The word carries powerful associations. To be at home is to feel at rest, safe, secure. Home is where we belong. To be away from home for long is to be displaced and uncertain.

The destruction of Jerusalem and the subsequent deportation of the Judeans finally occurred in 586 B.C. Nebuchadnezzar and his Babylonian army did what Jeremiah threatened they would do. King Zedekiah watched as his sons were killed by the Babylonians. He was then blinded and carried in chains to Babylon, along with the leading citizens. There was, for the exiles, literally no home left. Gone were "the house of the LORD, the king's house, and all the houses of Jerusalem; every great house [was] burned down" (2 Kin. 25:9). The walls, palace, and most importantly, the Temple—the glory of Solomon and the dwelling place of Yahweh—were no more.

The word of God had not been heeded. The Exile, or Babylonian Captivity, forced a realignment of Israel's understanding of who they were and who God would be for them. In their oracles to the exiles, Jeremiah and Ezekiel proclaimed that a new vision was taking shape in the heart of God. Another type of literature, the stories of Jonah, Ruth, and Esther, wrestles with the issue of what the relationship of the chosen people is to the foreign nations of the world. How Yahweh will dwell with the Jews and how the Jews will dwell in an often hostile world are the focal issues of this week's readings.

DAILY ASSIGNMENTS

As you read the Scriptures this week, keep in mind the following questions:
(1) How will God deal with the chosen people in the future, after the Exile?
(2) What attitudes do the chosen people have toward foreigners after the Exile?
(3) How do you account for the different perspectives on foreigners?

DAILY PRAYER PSALM: Psalm 137:1–6

DAY ONE: Jeremiah 1; 9; 18–20

What difficulties does Jeremiah experience as a prophet, or mouthpiece, for God? How do the various images of the potter, clay, and pots reflect the messages Jeremiah is called to deliver?

DAY TWO: Jeremiah 29–32

This section of what is sometimes called the "Little Book of Comfort" makes some amazing promises on God's part for the future. List the ones that most captured your attention.

13⁷ -24

DAY THREE: Ezekiel 1–3; 18; 34; 36–37

Ezekiel is the recipient of strange, even eerie visions, as well as of new teachings about God's ways in the future. Note the vivid imagery he uses. What features of his message do you think would capture the attention of the exiled Jews?

DAY FOUR: Esther

Esther and Mordecai triumph against all odds. With this book as your source, what is life like for Jews living in a foreign land?

DAY FIVE: Jonah; Ruth

The Ninevites are quick to receive the message of the reluctant prophet Jonah. The Moabite woman Ruth makes a way for herself and her mother-in-law, Naomi. What do these two stories together say about foreigners? About God's attitude toward those "outside" Israel?

DAY 6: Commentary

Read the commentary in the participant book.

JEREMIAH, PROPHET OF GOD'S HEART

Jeremiah's career spanned the turbulent years 627 to 587 B.C., during which three kings attempted various strategies to deal with the "foe from the North," the Neo-Babylonian Empire. Like Assyria two centuries before, Babylonia sought expansion out of Mesopotamia toward the trade routes along the Mediterranean Sea, and Judah was in the way. Judah was bullied first with forced tribute payments, then with deportation to Babylon when those tributes were withheld. Actually, two deportations occurred. The first, in 597, confirmed Jeremiah's prophecy of doom as the leading citizens were carried off to Babylon; then a puppet king, Zedekiah, was installed on the Judean throne. Barely ten years elapsed before the war party in Jerusalem again called for the overthrow of the Babylonian yoke, again against Jeremiah's counsel. The last and final deportation of 586 was the consequence.

> **Jeremiah's mission was chosen for him. The task for which he was born did not depend on his choice, but on God's.**

All the while, Jeremiah cajoled the people to repent and obey God, making predictions of doom and destruction and suffering punishment for his prophecies. The son of a priest from the city of Anathoth in the territory of Benjamin, Jeremiah was an outsider to the Jerusalem establishment. His only authority was his call from God, which comes at the beginning of the prophetic collection (Jer. 1:4-19). There we see features similar to the call of Moses: both Jeremiah and Moses protest that they are not up for the task; yet neither is allowed to back out. Remarkably, Jeremiah is told by God, "Before I formed you in the womb I knew you, / and before you were born I consecrated you; / I appointed you a prophet to the nations" (Jer. 1:5). His mission was chosen for him. The task for which he was born does not depend on his choice, but on God's.

Jeremiah's mission is twofold. Using strong images, Yahweh tells Jeremiah that he has been appointed to destroy and overthrow, as well as to build and plant (Jer. 1:10). It is important to keep this twofold mission in mind as we read the oracles in the text. Jeremiah's message is certainly one of judgment, of tearing down. Prior to the destruction of Jerusalem and the second deportation of 586, Jeremiah (like Amos) is a prophet of doom. But after 586, his message serves to rebuild the shattered hope of the people, offering them words of restoration and consolation.

Prior to seeing his people marched off into exile, Jeremiah speaks as if he knows the very heart of God. Like Hosea who married Gomer, their failed marriage a living parable of Israel's abandonment of God, Jeremiah also experiences the pain and heartache of God. The oracles of Jeremiah 9 are stormy judgments of Judah's apostasy. But the storm is a metaphor for God's tears (9:1, 10), which gush forth like rain from the heavens. Call for the mourning women, God cries. Have them raise a dirge. Their wailing will cover the grief of God so that it might flow freely: "that our eyes may run down with tears, / and our eyelids flow with water" (Jer. 9:17-18).

Years later, in his "Little Book of Comfort" (Jer. 29–33), addressed to the exiles in Babylon, Jeremiah at last proclaims the coming days of building and planting. God's judgment has passed and renewal and restoration will occur. In the future, God will make a new covenant with the people. The problem has been in the heart of Israel, which had broken God's heart. The prophet's call is for an internal and radical change: "I will give them one heart and one way, that they may fear me for all time, for their own good and the good of their children after them" (Jer. 32:39). The new covenant Jeremiah speaks of is not new in content; the intent is still the same: "I will be their God, and they shall be my people" (Jer. 31:33). But the agreement made at the time of Moses, a covenant that had repeatedly failed, will finally be realized. This time the law will be written not on tablets of stone, but on the heart. And this time, the covenant will not depend on Israel's obedience, but on God's forgiveness: "I will . . . remember their sin no more" (Jer. 31:34).

Yahweh had not abandoned his people. They were in exile and suffering the consequences of the broken covenant. But restoration of the covenant and of the Jews to their homeland was on the horizon. God was finding a new way to relate to God's people.

EZEKIEL, PROPHET OF GOD'S VISION

A contemporary of Jeremiah, Ezekiel was taken from Jerusalem to Babylon in 597 in the first of the two deportations. As a member of this first group of exiles, Ezekiel became their prophetic "pastor." When the exilic community learned of the destruction of Jerusalem in 586, the prophet mourned its loss along with the people. However, God had a new vision for the people and charged Ezekiel with communicating it to the people. Ezekiel presented a vision of what the survivors must do to rebuild their identity.

Ezekiel's most powerful image of the future restoration of his people is the vision of the valley of dry bones (Ezek. 37). Transported to a huge graveyard filled with dry carcasses, Ezekiel is ordered to prophesy to the bones. As he preached, the bones began to rattle and come together into skeletons. Ligaments formed, then skin, then the spirit or breath of Yahweh entered them. They lived and stood on their feet, a vast multitude. The dry bones represented Israel in exile. The word of God promised to bring them back to life, that is, to return them to their land and to restore them to a right relationship with their God. This vivid image of dead bones brought to life was a dramatic assurance that Israel's God was still present even when Israel's people were suffering and scattered. And it was a profound encouragement to Israel to look forward to certain restoration in the future and to remain faithful in the meantime.

Like Jeremiah, Ezekiel preaches that radical changes will be brought about by God in the future. In the past, Israel had blamed their problems on earlier generations. "The parents have eaten sour grapes, and the children's teeth are set on edge," they claimed (Ezek. 18:2). The children were suffering, not for their own disobedience, but for the sins of their parents. No longer will you quote this proverb, Ezekiel says (18:3; see also Jer. 31:27-30). Yahweh knows each person individually and will judge each generation by its own merits. "The righteousness of the righteous shall be his own, and the wickedness of the wicked will be his own" (Ezek. 18:20). Each generation has reason to hope because each will take responsibility for change and action. There is no room for fatalism, for making excuses and casting blame. The future is open-ended because God will start anew with the covenant in each generation. Again, like Jeremiah, Ezekiel knows that an internal change is necessary. Israel has a stubborn and hardened heart (Ezek. 3:7). Divine surgery, a transplant, is called for. And this is what Yahweh will do: "A new heart I will give you, and a new spirit I will put within you" (36:26). God will remove the heart of stone and give Israel a new heart of flesh that will be open and receptive to God.

> **Each generation has reason to hope because each will take responsibility for change and action. There is no room for fatalism, for making excuses and casting blame. The future is open-ended because God will start anew with the covenant in each generation.**

ISRAEL'S ROLE:
EXCLUSIVE OR INCLUSIVE?

After 539 B.C., Jews (the people of Judah, later Judea) were allowed to return to the Promised Land, to rebuild Jerusalem and a Second Temple. But Jewish communities still existed in foreign lands; those living in these communities were known as "Diaspora" Jews or people of the dispersion. Several texts of Scripture emerged to address some of the questions asked by these communities. For instance, What is the role of God's people, both Diaspora and resettled Jews, going forward? How should these Jews relate to the other nations of the earth?

The stories of Esther, Ruth, and Jonah were compiled after the Exile. Each story was originally set in a faraway time or place. Ruth is purportedly a story from the time of the judges. Esther is set in Persia during the reign of Xerxes (4 86 to 465 B.C.). Jonah cannot be dated with any certainty, although it tells the story of a prophet in Nineveh, the capital of the hated Assyrian Empire. Each story, in its own way, wrestles with the issue of how Israel is to relate to foreign peoples. Are they friends or foes? Part of God's plan, or threats to God's purposes?

> ### Diaspora Jews
>
>
> The Greek term, *diaspora*, meaning "scattered abroad," refers to those Jews who settled outside the land of Israel following the Babylonian exile (586 B.C.). According to the *Dictionary of Judaism in the Biblical Period* (Neusner and Green), rabbinic Judaism viewed the Diaspora both as punishment for the people's sin (a temporary suffering) and as the defining feature of Jewish life well into the future. This resulted in the development of rituals and communal practices appropriate for a Judaism no longer defined solely by the Temple and the land.

ESTHER

The story of Esther is set in Susa, the winter palace of the kings of the Achaemenid Empire of the Persian period. Esther was a Jewish orphan raised by her uncle, Mordecai. She became queen to Ahasuerus (Xerxes) by winning a beauty contest. However, Esther concealed her Jewish identity until the very end of the story. There was evidently a smoldering resentment against the large community of Diaspora Jews in Persia. The villain, Prime Minister Haman, was able to plot a pogrom, or slaughter, of all Jews in the empire. But his plans are overturned by our heroine. Esther is counseled by Mordecai in veiled, indirect language. He tells her that help will surely come from "another quarter" but, "who knows? Perhaps you have come to royal dignity for such a time as this" (Esth. 4:13-14).

The name of God does not appear in the entire book, reflecting dangerous times in which Jews must keep their identity secret. But the story's message strongly cautions the Jews that while enemies are all about, assimilation is not an option. God will provide, power plays will be thwarted, and hostile foreigners will ironically be overturned. Purim, the holiday that commemorates Esther and Mordecai's victory over Haman, celebrates Jewish identity and God's preservation of the Jews as a people.

RUTH

While the Book of Esther calls attention to the serious threats God's people face when living in an alien culture, the story of Ruth gives us another perspective on foreign peoples. Ruth is a Moabite; it is she who must cope with another culture. The Moabites were traditional enemies of Israel, especially in the exilic and postexilic periods. Yet her simple story is clearly told to set an example for Israel of goodness and courage. The famous declaration, often quoted in marriage ceremonies by the bride to the groom, is actually the widow Ruth's words to her Jewish mother-in-law, Naomi: "Where you go, I will go; / Where you lodge, I will lodge; / your people shall be my people, / and your God my God" (Ruth 1:16).

Ruth goes to great lengths to support Naomi. At Naomi's suggestion, she risks her physical safety in Boaz's fields and then risks everything when she offers herself to him on the threshing floor. She is rewarded with marriage to Boaz and a grandchild for Naomi. The addition of Ruth 4:17-22 expands the meaning of the simple story to show that foreigners are crucial to God's plan. The Moabite Ruth becomes the great-grandmother of Israel's greatest king, David. Were it not for the loyalty of this foreigner, the royal messianic line of David would not have existed.

JONAH

The Book of Jonah goes a step further in showing God's purposes for foreigners. Jonah is a reluctant prophet who is told to go prophesy to Nineveh, capital of the hated Assyrian Empire. But he instead heads in the exact opposite direction, toward Tarshish (Spain). Aboard ship, Jonah makes himself scarce while the sailors pray to their gods during a violent storm. Once the sailors determine that Jonah is the cause of the storm, these pagans actually begin to pray to God and do their best to save Jonah. Foreigners are also worthy of God's love!

After he finally arrives in Nineveh, Jonah hurriedly and halfheartedly calls on the Ninevites to repent. This they do wholeheartedly, from the king down to the livestock, and God decides not to destroy them. Jonah is resentful, even furious, and accuses God of being too merciful: You are gracious and merciful and abounding in love! he sneers (Jon. 4:2). The story is a satire of Jewish exclusivism. Jonah doesn't want God's mercy to extend to foreigners, yet the sailors and the Ninevites are quick to respond to the slightest suggestion that Jonah's God might be their God as well. While the Book of Esther advises "us" to be aware of "them" in a hostile world, the books of Jonah and Ruth make the case for the inclusion of foreigners in God's merciful calling.

INVITATION TO DISCIPLESHIP

At times, the very idea that God has a new vision is difficult to conceive. The world turns and our lives plod along. What could possibly change, and for the better at that? The story of Israel's Exile reminds us that the world seems to have a way of making exiles of people. Even a people bound by a covenant and promised a land can end up wayward and unfaithful as often as not. The experiences of suffering, loss, and displacement are common to us all. The story of the prophets of the Exile tells us that God is there even in those experiences. In the sometimes dark and distant places of our life journeys, God is preparing new things and promising new hope, new abundance, and new homecomings. The story of the prophets of the Exile is that God will go to great lengths and take radically bold measures to open our hearts, even while declaring that "your ways and your doings have brought this upon you" (Jer. 4:18). Through God's grace, what looked dry and brittle, like the valley of bones in Ezekiel's vision, can become vibrant, vital, and alive once again.

> **The story of Israel's Exile reminds us that the world seems to have a way of making exiles of people. Even a people bound by a covenant and promised a land can end up wayward and unfaithful as often as not.**

Important to remember, though, is that as God is doing this work, we have a responsibility and a role to play. Self-pity, fatalism, and blaming others are bankrupt strategies. We do well to be wary of outsiders (as Esther), but there is also another perspective we do well to embrace: those who are not "one of us" can teach us what God wants of us. God's purpose for God's chosen people, while special, is not necessarily exclusive. It may include the devotion of a Moabite widow or the edict of a mighty Persian king. For God is always and everywhere doing a new thing.

FOR REFLECTION

• Read aloud Psalm 137:1-4. In light of your study this week, how do these verses reflect the theme of the Scriptures you read? How is the voice of the text calling you to respond?

• What features of Jeremiah's and Ezekiel's messages speak most vividly to you?

• Reflect on your own experiences of suffering, loss, and displacement. How and when did God's word of hope break through?

DIGGING DEEPER

Do some research on the city of Nineveh, capital of the Assyrian Empire. What were the Ninevites like? How does that information put into context Jonah's initial reaction to God's call to preach to the inhabitants of Nineveh?

Read articles in a Bible dictionary or other resource about Nebuchadnezzer, the Babylonian Captivity, Cyrus the Great, Persia, and the Diaspora.

Restoration and Renewal

*For I am about to create new heavens / and a new earth; the former
things shall not be remembered / or come to mind.*

—*Isaiah 65:17*

INTRODUCTION

The biblical texts in this week's readings date from the periods known as the Restoration and Second Temple Judaism. Around 540 B.C., Jews in exile heard the words of comfort delivered by Second Isaiah (chapters 40–55). The prophet declared that God would bring God's people back home in what would be a new and glorious exodus. Once back in Judea, the governor, Nehemiah, and the priest, Ezra, promoted the rebuilding of Jerusalem and the renewal of the Mosaic covenant. Restoration prophets Haggai and Malachi urged the people to rebuild the Temple and purify themselves of foreign influences. While this perspective stands in contrast to the message of a book like Jonah (read last week), it is worth bearing in mind that resolving the problem of Israel's embrace of foreign cultures and their gods was of primary concern to the returning exiles.

The Hebrew Bible offers three different visions for the future. One view, put forth by Ezra and Nehemiah, represents a political program for national survival: if the Jews were to survive, they believed that it would be as a nation set apart by renewed adherence to the Torah. Another view, called "apocalyptic," offered by the Book of Daniel, looks forward to God's intervention in history. Cosmic warfare between great and opposing powers will result in a heavenly solution to earthly problems. Second and Third Isaiah (40–66) represent a third view. There the vision is global in scope and universal in mission. Israel's task is to serve the entire world as a "light to the nations."

DAILY ASSIGNMENTS

As you read through each passage of Scripture this week, keep in mind the following questions: (1) What is Isaiah's vision of the future? (2) How do the Jews srruggle with their restoration to their homeland after the Exile? (3) There are a variety of answers to the question: What next? What possible paths are delineated at the end of the history found in the Hebrew Bible?

DAILY PRAYER PSALM: Psalm 96

DAY 1: Isaiah 40–45; 49

Take note of the prophet's words of comfort. Notice the passages that show how the "God of Israel" is understood to be the One God of the universe.

broadcast – I will be salvation
Isreal w/ be a leader

DAY 2: Isaiah 50–55; 60; 65–66

What is the role of God's "servant"? What plans does God have for Israel and the rest of the nations?

follow God's Law –
enemy who doesn't worship God

DAY 3: Ezra 1; 3; 6; 9; Nehemiah 1; 2; 8–9; 13

Note the various efforts to restore the community in Jerusalem after the Exile. How did the leadership attempt to keep Judaism alive as a covenant religion?

DAY 4: Haggai; Malachi

List some of the concerns of these prophets. How does their message compare with that found in your Isaiah readings?

DAY 5: Daniel 7; 12

What are some of the key features of these apocalyptic visions?

a conversation *what we know*
of what we
cannot know

DAY 6: Commentary

Read the commentary in the participant book.

Note: *Because the voice of wisdom in the Hebrew Bible is not dealt with in this session's commentary, it is the subject of Part 1 of the video presentation. So to be prepared to discuss that video, read Job 7; Proverbs 2–3; and Ecclesiastes 3–4.*

A LIGHT TO THE NATIONS

The anonymous poet/prophet of chapters 40–55 in the present Book of Isaiah (referred to as Second Isaiah) lived among the Jewish exiles in Babylon and wrote around 540 B.C., on the eve of the fall of Babylon to King Cyrus of Persia. In perhaps some of the most poetic oracles in the Hebrew Bible, this anonymous author calls the people to rejoice over what God was planning to do for them and for all the nations of the earth.

Israel's audience felt that God had forsaken them in this strange land. However, the poet reminds them of the depths of God's love and care for them: "Can a woman forget her nursing child?.../ I have inscribed you on the palms of my hands" (Isa. 49:15-16). "My steadfast love shall not depart from you, / and my covenant of peace shall not be removed, / says the LORD" (54:10). The poet/prophet of Second Isaiah was called to comfort Israel with the good news that God was about to end the Exile. God would bring them home.

Central to Isaiah's theology is the understanding that the Holy One of Israel is also the Lord of all creation. Because God had shown the power of his word in the first creation of the universe, this same God could form a "new thing" out of the stuff of the universe (Isa. 41:17-20). In this new creation, the wilderness will become an Eden and the desert like a garden of the Lord (51:2-3). Because God is Lord of history and because God had shown mighty acts in the Exodus from Egypt, this same God could lead his people out of captivity yet a second time (43:16-21; 49:8-13).

Isaiah reminds Israel of the covenants with Abraham (Isa. 41:8; 51:2) and with David (55:3). Those were particular covenants with particular people. In God's threefold promise to Abraham, God swore that by (or through) Abraham, all the families of the earth would be blessed (Gen. 12:2; 22:18). To David, God swore that God would establish his house forever (2 Sam. 7). Second Isaiah develops these promises, beginning with Israel and extending into the entire world. The everlasting covenant with David is applied to Israel for this task: "See, you shall call nations that you do not know, / and nations that do not know you shall run to you, / because of the LORD your God" (Isa. 55:5). God's people will serve as a light to the nations, given by God as a covenant to all peoples (42:6), so that God's salvation or deliverance would shine out to the very ends of the earth.

What does it mean for Israel to serve as a light to the nations? It is through Israel that the righteousness of God was first made known. It is by Israel that God's ways of peace and justice will be made known to all peoples. Israel is like the funnel through which the One God of the universe pours blessing out into the world. For Second Isaiah, the goal of God's design is universal: "Listen to me, my people, / and give heed to me, my nation; / for a teaching will go out from me, / and my justice for a light to the peoples" (51:4). Love God and love the neighbor. As Jesus later pointed out, the Torah is distilled in these two great commandments. This teaching will shine forth to all the nations. What are the means by which God will accomplish this task? First, in the immediate future, God would equip and use a foreigner "who knows him not" (45:5). The Persian king, Cyrus, would issue an edict of liberation (538 B.C.), allowing all exiled peoples to return to their homelands and rebuild their cities. Later, at some unspecified time in the future, God would call a "servant" to bring forth truth and justice. In what scholars refer to as the "Suffering Servant" songs, in Second Isaiah, we find four poems that are concerned with the future of Israel and of the world (42:1-4; 49:1-6; 50:4-11; 52:13–53:12).

> **What does it mean for Israel to serve as a light to the nations? It is through Israel that the righteousness of God was first made known. It is by Israel that God's ways of peace and justice will be made known to all peoples.**

The identity of the servant, or servants, is not clear. In some cases the servant appears to be the nation Israel, in other cases an individual or a prophetic figure. The texts tell us that great service to the world will be accomplished only by great sacrifice. The servant will suffer vicariously, on behalf of others, to accomplish God's design in history. God's salvation is delivered to all peoples through the way of selflessness, rather than through the sword of military might.

RESTORATION IN THE LAND OF PROMISE

Seven hundred years after the Exodus, the returning exiles once again entered the Promised Land. They returned in waves and rebuilt in fits and starts. Notice that the books of Ezra and Nehemiah do not read chronologically. One possible arrangement of the passages, which have been dislocated in transmission, has a first wave coming back to a devastated Jerusalem around 538 B.C. and laying the foundations for the Second Temple on top of the ruins of Solomon's (first) Temple (Ezra 1–6). Political troubles brought the project to a halt until the prophet Haggai called for the rebuilding to continue (about 520). Haggai demanded an accounting from his audience. While they lived in paneled houses and took care of themselves, the house of the Lord lay in ruins (Hag. 1:4). Haggai urges them to resume their work on the rebuilding, and they will be blessed (2:6-9). Haggai expressed the priestly perspective that national prosperity depended on the Lord's presence in Jerusalem and the belief that the Lord would not return without a dwelling place, the Temple. Work began again, and in 515 B.C., the Second Temple was completed.

Some time after the Temple was completed, around 444 B.C., Nehemiah arrived in Jerusalem. As governor of Judah, he was responsible for rebuilding the city walls around Jerusalem (Neh. 1–7). Despite opposition from outside enemies, Nehemiah's crew was able to complete the walls in fifty-two days. These walls gave Jerusalem much-needed protection and security. Ezra, the great priest and scribe of the Restoration, probably came to Jerusalem around 458. Under Ezra, the Jews rededicated themselves to the Mosaic covenant (Ezra 9; Neh. 8–9). Both Ezra and Nehemiah called for foreigners to be separated from the covenant community. This meant the annulment of mixed marriages with foreigners (Neh. 13; Ezra 9) as well as no future intermarriage.

Nehemiah's brick wall around Jerusalem and Ezra's "hedge" of the Torah around the Jews were both ways to reestablish and maintain Jewish identity. Membership in the covenant community would thereafter be determined by two things: the observance of Torah (law) and the birthright of Jewish descent. To keep the people pure, sacrifices were offered once again in the Second Temple. Henceforth, the priests would lead the community while the scribes and rabbis would teach the legally correct religious practices: dietary laws, tithes, observance of the sabbath, and annual festivals. The covenant community delivered out of slavery, that had for a brief time become a nation, now just returned from exile, would begin the hard work of reconstructing its identity all over again.

AN APOCALYPTIC END

Now fast-forward from the time of Ezra and Nehemiah to 331 B.C. when Alexander the Great toppled the Persian Empire. When Alexander died eight years later without an heir, his lands were divided among his generals; and Judah, renamed Palestine, eventually came to be controlled by the Seleucid family. Antiochus IV was a Seleucid, a Hellenized king who hated his Jewish subjects. He set up an altar to Zeus in the Second Temple of Jerusalem, ordered Jews to eat swine's flesh in violation of their dietary laws, forbade circumcision, and put to death those who possessed the Torah.

Around 167 B.C., Antiochus's blasphemous policies prompted an insurgence by loyal Jews, called the Maccabean Revolt. These loyal Jews were called Hasids, "faithful ones." Their political struggle is recounted in First and Second Maccabees in the Apocrypha section of the Bible. The Revolt ended with the cleansing of the Temple and its rededication in 164 in an eight-day celebration called Hanukkah.

It was most likely during these turbulent times that the largest and best example of apocalyptic writing in the Hebrew Bible, Daniel 7–12, was written. Unlike the first section of the book (Dan. 1–6), a set of hero stories set during the Babylonian period, the last section calls on Israel to look beyond their suffering to a glorious future in the hands of God. History, according to Daniel, is heading toward culmination in the heavenly kingdom. God will intervene, soon and catastrophically, on behalf of God's people.

Apocalyptic writings were addressed to an audience undergoing suffering and persecution. Dreams, visions, animal symbols, and numerical codes are stock features of this kind of writing. The authorities would not be able to understand the cryptic language or decipher the puzzles, but the Jews could find the real message.

Daniel 7, as a prime example of apocalyptic symbolism, depicts a vision of four beasts, each representing the great empires of the Ancient Near East. The winged lion is the Babylonian Empire; the bear is the Median Empire; the winged leopard the Persian

> ### Dating Daniel
>
>
>
> Many scholars argue for dating the writing of Daniel during the second century B.C., even though the stories are set in sixth century Babylon. Historical inaccuracies in chapters 1–6 (e.g., Nabonidus was the father of Belshazzar, not Nebuchadnezzer) and the more accurate descriptions of the persecution of Antiochus IV in chapter 11 are cited as evidence in support of the second century B.C. date. The Hebrew Bible puts Daniel after Esther in the *Kethuvim*, reflecting the Babylonian setting of the narratives. The Christian Bible, on the other hand, retains the ordering of the Septuagint, placing Daniel as the last of the major prophets.

Empire; and the beast with iron teeth is the empire of Alexander the Great. The ten horns of the fourth beast, Persia, represent his Seleucid successors, and the little horn with eyes is the tyrannical king of Palestine, Antiochus. In this vision a magnificent figure, called the "Ancient One," comes in glory to judge with his mighty court of thousands. Following the destruction of the fourth beast, a kingdom is instituted for all eternity, an "everlasting kingdom." A "son of man," or "one like a human being," is given eternal kingship by the Ancient One; and all peoples, nations, and languages will serve him. The human-like figure symbolizes the collective people of God, just as the beasts each stood for an empire. The "holy ones," as they are called, come to possess the kingdom of God for all time.

Daniel 12 envisions the final consummation of history. The angel, Michael, of this chapter is the patron angel of the Jews. Note that the writer himself is assured a place in the end of days and the beginning of God's eternal reign (12:3). Notice also that his words are to be sealed up and kept secret until the end times (12:4, 9). Whereas prophetic literature of the Hebrew Bible is to be broadcast and proclaimed, apocalypses are veiled and hidden. They are also pessimistic about the role of human agency and its structures in successfully battling evil. The eternal kingdom will come at last, after great turmoil, only by the intervention of God. The message to the faithful is to endure in times of political crisis and to put their hope in the power of God's rule.

INVITATION TO DISCIPLESHIP

The Hebrew Bible leaves us with three visions: the heavenly/apocalyptic view of Daniel—"The kingship and dominion / and the greatness of the kingdoms under the whole heaven / shall be given to the people of the holy ones of the Most High" (Dan. 7:27); the earthly/political solution of restoration in the fashion of Nehemiah—"Then those of Israelite descent separated themselves from all foreigners, and stood and confessed their sins and the iniquities of their ancestors" (Neh. 9:2); and the universal/global mission of Isaiah—"Turn to me and be saved, / all the ends of the earth! / For I am God, and there is no other" (Isa. 45:22). Each vision represents a slightly different perspective on the role of human agency and the action of God in ushering in God's future.

We turn to Scripture at times for immediate guidance and at other points in our lives for long-range visions. Sometimes we are like the Jews, who on their return to Jerusalem, heard Ezra's call to preserve their identity and establish themselves as a people. At other times, we might pray for divine intervention and for imaginative pictures, like apocalypses, of real and lasting change in the stories of our lives that only God can bring about. Finally there is the goal of *tikkun olam,* Hebrew for "healing the world." Perhaps that is the best way of all to say what these Scriptures invite us to know and live out. For ultimately, this story is about God from beginning to end: God's blessing of Creation, God's promise to Abraham, God's deliverance of the Hebrews, God's giving of the Law, God's faithfulness in spite of the people's faithlessness, and God's vision of restoration. The invitation to us, then, is to help God finish the story.

FOR REFLECTION

• Read aloud Isaiah 65:17. In light of your study this week, how does this verse reflect the theme of the Scriptures you read? How is the voice of the text calling you to respond?

• Of the three visions (Daniel, Ezra/Nehemiah, Isaiah), which most closely represents how you see God's vision for the future?

• To what extent has your image of the future of God's people (end of time) changed over the years? Is that image influenced more by the Old Testament or the New Testament? Why is that?

DIGGING DEEPER

Locate a copy of the Dead Sea Scrolls in English (see the bibliography on page 10), and read several of the nonbiblical passages, especially The Community Rule and the War Scroll. Read articles about the Qumran community and Qumran perspectives on end times, the nature of the Messiah, and Jewish funeral practices.

Consider how findings related to Qumran inform our understanding of Judaism and early Christianity.

Video Art Credits

OPENING SEQUENCE

First Isaiah Scroll / Photo by John Trevers / Biblical Archaeological Society ❖ *The Ancient of Days* by William Blake. British Museum, London / SuperStock ❖ *The Departure of Abraham* by Josef Molnar. National Gallery, Budapest, Hungary/ ET Archive, London / SuperStock ❖ *Moses and the Children of Israel* by Richard McBee © Richard McBee. Used by permission of the artist. ❖ *The Destruction of the Temple of Jerusalem, Detail showing the menorah of the Temple* by Francesco Hayez. Cameraphoto / Art Resource, NY ❖ *The Prophet Jeremiah Lamenting the Destruction of Jerusalem* by Rembrandt van Rijn. Rijksmuseum, Amsterdam, Netherlands / SuperStock ❖ First Isaiah Scroll / Photo by John Trevers / Biblical Archaeological Society

ART PANELS

The Ancient of Days by William Blake. British Museum, London / SuperStock ❖ *Losing Paradise* © He Qi. Used by permission of the artist. ❖ *The Departure of Abraham* by Josef Molnar. National Gallery, Budapest, Hungary / ET Archive, London / SuperStock ❖ *Moses and the Children of Israel* by Richard McBee © Richard McBee. Used by permission of the artist. ❖ *The Ark at the Nile* by James Jacques Tissot. The Jewish Museum, NY / Art Resource, NY ❖ *King David on Red Ground* by Marc Chagall. Réunion des Musées Nationaux / Art Resource, NY © 2005 Artists Rights Society (ARS), New York / ADAGP, Paris ❖ *The Visit of the Queen of Sheba to King Solomon* by Edward John Poynter. Art Gallery of New South Wales, Sydney, Australia / SuperStock ❖ *The Destruction of the Temple of Jerusalem, Detail showing the Menorah of the Temple* by Francesco Hayez. Cameraphoto / Art Resource, NY ❖ *The Prophet Jeremiah Lamenting the Destruction of Jerusalem* by Rembrandt van Rijn. Rijksmuseum, Amsterdam, Netherlands / SuperStock ❖ *Belshazzar's Feast* by Rembrandt van Rijn. National Gallery, London, Great Britain / Art Resource, NY

TEXTILE ART

Banners by Sandra Briney Designs, 512 East Broadway Avenue, Medford, Wisconsin 54451 (www.sbweavingdesigns.com)

VIDEO CREDITS

SEGMENT 1

Part 1: Torah Scroll from which the daily chapter is read in the Synagogue © Zev Radovan

Part 2: Leningrad Codex. Photograph by Bruce and Kenneth Zuckerman, West Semitic Research in collaboration with the Ancient Biblical Manuscript Center. Manuscript located in the Russian National Library in St. Petersburg. ❖ Silver Amulet with Priestly Blessing / Photo by Zev Radovan / Biblical Archaeological Society ❖ First Isaiah Scroll / Photo by John Trevers / Biblical Archaeological Society ❖ "Lost" Fragment of Samuel / Photo courtesy of the Israel Antiquities Authority / Biblical Archaeological Society

SEGMENT 2

Part 1: *The Caravan of Abraham* by James Jaques Tissot. Photo Credit: The Jewish Museum, NY / Art Resource, NY ❖ Jacob's Blessing by Rembrandt van Rijn. Staatliche Kunstsammlung Kassel, Germany / AKG Berlin / SuperStock ❖ *Abraham Turning Away Hagar* by Emile Jean Horace Vernet. Museé des Beaux-Arts, Nantes, France / Bridgeman Art Library ❖ Lines from Scroll of Isaiah found in the cave of Qumran. Israel Museum (IDAM), Jerusalem, Israel. Erich Lessing / Art Resource, NY ❖ The Codex Sinaiticus, Greek Bible, 4th C. British Library, London, Great Britain. HIP / Art Resource, NY ❖ Page from the Koran (15th C). Réunion des Museés Nationaux / Art Resource, NY

Part 2: *Sacrifice of Isaac* by Felice Ficherelli. Private Collection © Bonhams, London, UK / Bridgeman Art Library ❖ Satellite Photograph of the Territory of Ancient Israel and Neighbors / National Aeronautics and Space Administration / Biblical Archaeological Society ❖ Map of the Ancient Near East / Biblical Archaeological Society ❖ The Ziggurat at Ur / Photo by Hirmer Verlag / Biblical Archaeological Society ❖ Ugaritic Relief of the Canaanite God EL / Photo by Erich Lessing / Biblical Archaeological Society ❖ Three Late Bronze Female Figures / Photo by Zev Radovan / Biblical Archaeological Society ❖ Cast Images / Photo by Zev Radovan / Biblical Archaeological Society ❖ Circumcision / Photo by Zev Radovan / Biblical Archaeological Society ❖ Late Bronze Cuneiform Writing on Tablet, Megiddo / Photo by Zev Radovan / Biblical Archaeological Society ❖ Tel Beersheba (Aerial) / Photo by Zev Herzog / Biblical Archaeological Society ❖ Middle Bronze I Round House, Negev / Photo by Jonathan Kline / Biblical Archaeological Society ❖ Reconstructed Roof of Round House / Photo by Jonathan Kline / Biblical Archaeological Society

SEGMENT 3

Part 1: *The Crossing of the Red Sea* by Marc Chagall. Réunion des Museés Nationaux / Art Resource, NY © 2005 Artists Rights Society (ARS), New York / ADAGP, Paris ❖ *Finding of Moses* © 2001, He Qi. Used by permission of artist. ❖ Seder Plate. Digital Vision, Ltd. / SuperStock ❖ *The Last Supper* by Sadao Watanabe © Asian Christian Artist Association

Part 2: Satellite Photograph of Sinai / Photo by NASA / Biblical Archaeological Society ❖ Brickmaking in Egypt / Photo by Erich Lessing / Biblical Archaeological Society ❖ Gathering Straw and Mud / Photo by Erich Lessing / Biblical Archaeological Society ❖ Brickmaking / Photo by Erich Lessing / Biblical Archaeological Society ❖ Burning Bush Mosaic / Photo by Fred Anderegg © National Geographic Society / Biblical Archaeological Society ❖ Acacia Trees in Eastern Sinai / Photo by Erich Lessing / Biblical Archaeological Society ❖ Pharaoh Ramesses II in His Chariot / Courtesy of the Oriental Institute of the University of Chicago / Biblical Archaeological Society ❖ Mummy of Pharaoh Ramesses II / Photo by Garo Nalbandian / Biblical Archaeological Society ❖ Map of Sinai and Negev / by Barry J. Beitzel, from *The Moody Atlas of Bible Lands* (Chicago: Moody Press, 1985) / Biblical Archaeological Society ❖ Monastery and Plain of er-Raha / Photo by Robert F. Sisson © National Geographic Society / Biblical Archaeological Society ❖ Jebel Serbal from Wadi Feiran / Photo by David Harris / Biblical Archaeological Society ❖ Bronze Bull Figurine / Photo by Zev Radovan / Biblical Archaeological Society ❖ Scene from the Code of Hammurabi / Photo by Erich Lessing / Biblical Archaeological Society

SEGMENT 4

Part 1: *The Seven Trumpets of Jericho* by James Jacques Tissot. The Jewish Museum, NY / Art Resource, NY ❖ *God Baal of the Thunderstorm, Gilded bronze idol.* Louvre, Paris, France. Erich Lessing / Art Resource, NY

Part 2: Map of Biblical Israel / Biblical Archaeological Society ❖ Merneptah Stela / Photo by Jürgen Liepe / Biblical Archaeological Society ❖ Mt. Ebal Installation / Photo by Adam Zertal / Biblical Archaeological Society ❖ Mt. Ebal Altar, Artist's Reconstruction / Drawing by Judith Dekel / Biblical Archaeological Society ❖ Near Eastern Tell / Photo by Zev Radovan / Biblical Archaeological Society ❖ Central Hills and Upland Valleys / Photo by Zev Radovan / Biblical Archaeological Society ❖ Philistine Pottery / Photo by Zev Radovan / Biblical Archaeological Society ❖ Pottery / Photo by Carl Andrews / Leon Levy Expedition to Ashkelon/ Biblical Archaeological Society ❖ Four-Room House / Photo by Zev Radovan / Biblical Archaeological Society ❖ Reconstruction Drawing of a Four-Room House / Reprinted from *The Oxford History of the Biblical World*, edited by Michael D. Coogan (Oxford University Press, 1998) / Biblical Archaeological Society

SEGMENT 5

Part 1: *Noah's Ark* by Edward Hicks. The Philadelphia Museum of Art / Art Resource, NY ❖ *The Departure of Abraham* by Josef Molnar. National Gallery, Budapest, Hungary/ ET Archive, London / SuperStock ❖ *The Ten Commandments* by Tadao Tanaka © Asian Christian Artist Association ❖ *King David on Red Ground* by Marc Chagall. Réunion des Musées Nationaux / Art Resource, NY © 2005 Artists Rights Society (ARS), New York / ADAGP, Paris

Part 2: Map: Jerusalem from Jebusites to Hezekiah / Adapted from *Carta's Historical Atlas of Jerusalem* by Dan Bahat © Carta 1983 / Biblical Archaeological Society ❖ Aerial Detail of Ophel Hill and Temple Mount / Photo by Zev Radovan / Biblical Archaeological Society ❖ Reconstruction of the Jerusalem Temple / Drawing by Leen Ritmeyer © Ritmeyer Archaeological Design / Biblical Archaeological Society ❖ Proto-Aeolic Capital / Photo by Zev Radovan / Biblical Archaeological Society ❖ Ophel Hill: Stepped-Structure / Photo by Raphael Magnes / Biblical Archaeological Society ❖ Iron II Israelite Pottery / Photo by Zev Radovan / Biblical Archaeological Society ❖ "House of David" Stela / Photo by Zev Radovan / Biblical Archaeological Society ❖ Shishak Relief at Karnak / Photo by Erich Lessing / Biblical Archaeological Society

SEGMENT 6

Part 1: *The Prophet Nathan Admonishes King David* by Palma Giovane. Kunsthistorisches Museum, Vienna, Austria. Erich Lessing / Art Resource, NY ❖ *Elijah Dwelleth in a Cave* by James Jacques Tissot. The Jewish Museum, NY / SuperStock

Part 2: Tel Dan, High Place / Photo by Zev Radovan / Biblical Archaeological Society ❖ Bronze Bull Figurine / Photo by Zev Radovan / Biblical Archaeological Society ❖ Palace of Ahab at Samaria / Photo by Zev Radovan / Biblical Archaeological Society ❖ Bronze Statuette of Ba'al / Photo by Zev Radovan / Biblical Archaeological Society ❖ Kuntillet 'Ajrud Graffito: "Yahweh and His Asherah" / Photo by Ze'ev Meshel / Biblical Archaeological Society ❖ Black Obelisk: Jehu Bowing Before Shalmaneser II / Photo by Erich Lessing / Biblical Archaeological Society ❖ Black Obelisk: Israelites Bringing Tribute / Photo by Erich Lessing / Biblical Archaeological Society ❖ The Siege of Lachish: Fighting from the Tower / Photo by Erich Lessing / Biblical Archaeological Society ❖ The Siege of Lachish: Dead Israelites / Photo by Erich Lessing / Biblical Archaeological Society ❖ Black Obelisk: Details of Tribute from Israel

/ Photo by Erich Lessing / Biblical Archaeological Society ❖ Iron II Water Tunnel / Photo by Hershel Shanks / Biblical Archaeological Society ❖ Hezekiah's Tunnel: Siloam Inscription / Photo by Zev Radovan / Biblical Archaeological Society ❖ Prism of Sennacherib, Nineveh / Photo courtesy of The Oriental Institute, University of Chicago/ Biblical Archaeological Society

SEGMENT 7

Part 1: Jewish Captives on Their Way to Exile, Detail of the Assyrian conquest of the Jewish town of Lachish. Relief from Palace of Sennacherib. British Museum, London. Erich Lessing / Art Resource, NY ❖ *By the Waters of Babylon* by Evelyn De Morgan. The De Morgan Centre, London. Bridgeman Art Library ❖ Torah Scroll, Parchment, Germany (15th) © Zev Radovan ❖ The Western wall of the Temple in Jerusalem, 7th BCE. Temple Mount, Jerusalem. Erich Lessing / Art Resource, NY

Part 2: Judean Pillar Figurines / Photo by David Harris / Biblical Archaeological Society ❖ Ishtar Gate, Babylon / Staatliche Museen zu Berlin, Preussischer Kulturbesitz, Vorderasiatisches Museum / Biblical Archaeological Society ❖ The Cyrus Cylinder / Photo courtesy of the Trustees of the British Museum / Biblical Archaeological Society ❖ Citadel at Persepolis / Photo by James Wellard / Sonia Halliday Photographs / Biblical Archaeological Society ❖ Persepolis: Darius on Throne / Photo by Zev Radovan / Biblical Archaeological Society

SEGMENT 8

Part 1: *The Creation of Light* by Gaetano Previati. Galleria Nazionale d'Arte Moderna, Rome. Scala / Art Resource, NY ❖ *Christ and His Mother* by Henry Ossawa Tanner. Dallas Museum of Art, Deaccession Funds ❖ *Job and the Whirlwind* by William Blake / SuperStock

Part 2: Jerusalem: Herod's Temple Mount / Drawing by Leen Ritmeyer / Biblical Archaeological Society ❖ Cave 1, General View, Limestone Cliffs / Photo by Zev Radovan / Biblical Archaeological Society ❖ Qumran Settlement, Aerial View / Photo by Werner Braun / Biblical Archaeological Society ❖ Manual of Discipline / Photo by John Trevers / Biblical Archaeological Society ❖ Replica of Community Rule ❖ War Scroll / Photo courtesy of the Israel Museum, Jerusalem / Shrine of the Book / Biblical Archaeological Society ❖ Mikveh / Photo by David Harris / Biblical Archaeological Society ❖ Cemetery / Photo by David Harris / Biblical Archaeological Society ❖ "Messiah Apocalypse" Fragment / Photo courtesy of the Ancient Biblical Manuscript Center / Israel Antiquities Authority / Biblical Archaeological Society